First in the World

FIRST IN THE WORLD

The story of the

National Youth Orchestra of Wales

BERYL BOWEN JAMES

and

DAVID IAN ALLSOBROOK

CARDIFF

UNIVERSITY OF WALES PRESS

1995

A catalogue record for this book is available from the British Library.

ISBN 0-7083-1296-9

Typeset at the University of Wales Press
Printed in Great Britain by Henry Ling Limited, at the The Dorset Press, Dorchester

This book is dedicated to Irwyn Ranald Walters who, in founding the National Youth Orchestra of Wales, enriched the lives of countless young instrumentalists in the principality. He initiated a new musical tradition in Wales, a country where the emphasis had previously been on the performance of vocal music.

Contents

Acknowledgements

Thanks are due to my family and all my friends for the help, encouragement and interest which they have shown in the production of this book. Many past members of the orchestra have contributed to the text in the form of signed reminiscences.

Irwyn Walters provided photographs, programmes and personal correspondence from friends and colleagues. I enjoyed many long conversations with Irwyn and his wife Meg, who herself was closely involved in all Irwyn's musical activities and had an amazing memory. I am also very grateful to Gareth, Irwyn's son, for all his help since Irwyn's death.

Kathryn Phipps was very generous in allowing me to use her scrapbooks and photographs. She was a cellist in the 1960s and is at present a housemistress with the orchestra.

I also owe a debt of gratitude to the following: A. J. Heward Rees and his assistants, Julie Wilcox and Siân Emlyn; the WJEC and their Administrator of the NYOW, Beryl Jones; and to the late Dorothy Adams-Jeremiah, Megan Mansel Thomas, Joyce Camden, Elizabeth Davison, Julie Evans, Mathew Evans, Lionel Salter, the late Leslie Tusler, the late Agnes McDonald and Mr and Mrs John Cynan Jones.

Beryl Bowen James

Introduction

The phenomenon of the youth orchestra is well-known but historically neglected. The most recent edition of *Grove's Dictionary of Music and Musicians* (1980) has neither an entry on 'youth orchestras' nor even a sub-section devoted to the subject under 'orchestra'. Such omissions may seem inexplicable, but they are part of the general mystification about processes of musical education. It is probable that many people who now enthusiastically buy classical CDs in vast quantities have never given a thought to the great accumulation of educational and professional experience which underpins every recorded and live orchestral performance. Even after some desultory thought they may imagine that professional players emerge fully formed at some misty post-adolescent moment, like Botticelli's Venus rising from a calm sea.

Over the past fifty years in Europe and America, there can be little doubt but that the youth orchestra movement has made the greatest single contribution to raising the quality of professional music-making. It has provided experience and appreciation of the highest performing standards, under the best conductors and instrumental coaches, encouraging countless youngsters to enter important careers in music and find fulfilment.

The National Youth Orchestra of Wales was *the very first* of these great institutions. Today it is an infectiously enthusiastic annual gathering of gifted young people, united in their love of music and the discipline of music-making. The orchestra, over nearly fifty years, has built for itself a reputation which far transcends the boundaries of Wales. Under a series of fine conductors – Clarence Raybould, Arthur Davison and now Elgar Howarth – it has heightened the musical experience of hundreds of youngsters and delighted audiences of hundreds of thousands in concert halls and through radio and television performances, nationally and internationally.

Such phenomena are never born spontaneously: generally their conception requires the prior vision and administrative qualities of one person. In the case of the National Youth Orchestra of Wales that individual was Irwyn Ranald Walters OBE, who died, in his ninetieth year, on 22 November 1992. Clarence Raybould, the orchestra's much respected first conductor, said of him: 'I would stress that he is the man responsible for the orchestra, because he had the vision to foresee it' (*Welsh Music*, II, 8, 1965, 18). And a Welsh music critic of the post-war years described Irwyn Walters as

> . . . the man who started a new musical tradition in Wales through his founding of the National Youth Orchestra . . . probably the most significant and spectacular innovation in Welsh music for centuries, which has changed the emphasis in music in Wales and provided a new medium for the display of Welsh talent. (Kenneth Loveland, 'The Welsh Musical Awakening', *Welsh Music*, II, 8, 1965, 18.)

Today the name of Irwyn Walters probably means as little to the general musical public as it does to current and recent members of the NYOW. It would be sad if that were to remain true. Accordingly we shall make an attempt, here, not only to record the great achievement of the founder of the orchestra, but to place it firmly in the context of musical and educational development in Britain and worldwide during the period since 1945.

David Allsobrook

I Origins

Irwyn Ranald Walters was born on 6 December 1902 in Amman-ford, in the old county of Carmarthenshire. The timing of his birth is significant since, at the beginning of this century, Wales was experiencing a broad cultural re-awakening. The country had acquired a national system of secondary or intermediate schooling in 1889; a national university with its own charter in 1893; a National Library and a National Museum in 1905. It was also a matter of considerable pride then that, of all the British peoples, the Welsh were the most musical, in the sense that they could sing in parts majestically and passionately; though as yet they seemed to lack both a strong orchestral tradition and a composer of international eminence.

Irwyn Walters was also fortunate in being born in Ammanford, a thriving industrial town which – like Aberdare, Mountain Ash, Merthyr Tydfil, Dowlais and Rhymney – was forging a reputation for an intense musicality which was dispersed widely among a largely working-class population. Musical expertise in Wales had been generated partly through an English educational invention, tonic sol-fa, developed by a Congregational minister, John Curwen (1816–1880). Curwen was able to write, in the introduction to his *Teacher's Manual* (1875), that 'there is no country so forward in Tonic Sol-fa as Wales'. And the statistical evidence shows that, by 1910, of the 500 licentiates of the Tonic Sol-fa College at Plaistow, more than 300 were Welsh. (See Gareth Williams, 'How's the tenors in Dowlais?': hegemony, harmony and popular culture in England and Wales, 1600–1900', *Llafur* 5, 1, 1988, 77.) Such bare facts should be enlarged by stating that those 300 were probably all teachers, in day schools, chapels, churches and Sunday schools, nurturing skills throughout the population on a vast scale.

It was mainly through the culture of Nonconformity – the chapels – that the mead of tonic sol-fa was dispensed. David Walters, Irwyn's grandfather, became an expert in the method, and he was the founder of the first oratorio choir in Ammanford. He transmitted his expertise to his son, William, Irwyn's father, who developed a resonant bass voice and became precentor of Ebenezer Baptist chapel, serving also as bass-leader in the great

Irwyn Ranald Walters, founder of the National Youth Orchestra of Wales.

Ammanford Choir, which won the Chief Choral at the National Eisteddfod in 1919 and 1920 under its inspirational conductor Gwilym R. Jones.

In those later years of Irwyn's boyhood, the Ammanford Choir was playing a leading role in the Welsh musical renaissance. In 1919 Walford Davies was appointed first director of the Welsh National Council of Music and first Gregynog Professor of Music at Aberystwyth University College. In the nineteenth century tonic sol-fa had tied the repertoire of Welsh choirs to a diet of Handel and Mendelssohn. Now, in the years immediately after the First World War, Walford Davies sought to introduce Welsh choralists to the glories of a European tradition of liturgical music which focused on the works of Bach and Brahms. Thus it was that the young Irwyn and his brothers were taken to hear the Ammanford Choir's performances of Brahms' 'German Requiem' and Bach's Mass in B minor. Such impressions marked out for Irwyn Walters the way he wanted to go. The other change which Walford Davies required of Welsh musicians after 1919 was that they should gain a greater, more universal measure of instrumental and orchestral expertise.

Irwyn's father, William Walters, began work as a boy in a

tinplate mill at Pantyffynnon; but ill health forced him to withdraw, and he opened a tobacconist's and newsagent's shop in The Square in Ammanford. In addition to William's musical ability and enthusiasm, his wife, Elizabeth, was the sister of the noted Welsh poet, William Morgan, whose bardic name was 'Rhandir'; and so family life was streaked through with cultural and aesthetic enthusiasm of a profoundly Welsh kind. Of the other five children, Merfyn became a cellist, while Hugh was to become a Baptist minister.

The lasting potency of early informal experience in musical education is often overlooked. Irwyn Walters emerged from a very musical home to begin his formal education in 1908 at Ammanford Council School. There, in the usual way, music played a peripheral part in the curriculum – the singing of a hymn at morning assembly and perhaps at the end of each school day. But, after successfully passing the scholarship examination to Ammanford Intermediate School in 1915, Irwyn experienced, perhaps more fruitfully than others in his generation, an expansion of formal musical training. He was fortunate that the music teacher who came in to give singing lessons under the requirements of the 1904 Board of Education *Regulations for Secondary Schools* was Gwilym R. Jones, conductor of the great Ammanford Choir.

Outside the limited formal curriculum, Gwilym Jones was also Irwyn's private piano and organ teacher. Eventually, he went for piano lessons in Swansea with Dr David Vaughan Thomas, the leading native Welsh musician of that time, a pianist, Eisteddfod adjudicator and composer of considerable eminence. There should have been great sympathy between the teacher, born in 1873, and the pupil, since Vaughan Thomas's mother was a native of Ammanford. Educated first in Pontarddulais, then Ammanford, Vaughan Thomas had so impressed his teachers that he won a prestigious scholarship to a 'nearby public school', Llandovery College, where he made such a mark on his peers that he was awarded the nickname 'Dai Piano'. He went up to Oxford University on a scholarship in 1898. There, though his specialism was mathematics, he joined the newly formed Oxford Musical Union, and, in association with Henry Hadow, Fellow of Worcester College and the first modern English musicologist, he began to play a leading pianistic role in performances of recent and contemporary chamber music. His first-class honours degree in mathematics took him to various middle-class schools in England, before he landed the post of Assistant Director of Music at Harrow School under Dr Percy Buck, another Oxford musician whose scholarship would mould musical taste and aspiration in Britain.

While teaching mathematics and music at Harrow, Vaughan Thomas submitted work to Oxford University which led to the award of a B. Mus. degree.

While at Oxford, however, David Vaughan Thomas had retained his Welsh identity, to the extent of joining the scholarly Dafydd ap Gwilym Society, which nurtured his deep and persisting love of Welsh medieval poetry. And his great longing was to return to Wales and use his musical talent and appreciation of Welsh poetry to transform the raw material of Welsh musicality into something which would transcend the currently complacent confidence in a native singing ability. In 1908 David Vaughan Thomas returned, to take up the post of choirmaster and organist at the Mount Pleasant chapel in Swansea. Subsequently for nearly thirty years he travelled all over Wales, spreading his gospel of a new spirit in Welsh music, adjudicating, encouraging other Welsh composers, organizing concerts and, above all, teaching. This was the highly gifted man who took over the early musical education of young Irwyn Walters and expanded his horizons. Years later, near the end of his life, Irwyn was to say of Vaughan Thomas: 'He gave me my first insight into the playing of Mozart.'

During the First World War, the Board of Education encouraged several progressive changes in the School Certificate examination system of secondary schools in England and Wales. Music, however, remained a peripheral subject, together with art, handicraft and domestic science. Nevertheless, Irwyn Walters's interest in music kindled his wish to study it as one of the subjects for the Higher School Certificate examination. With the help of Gwilym R. Jones, and the acquisition of the necessary texts, he became the first Ammanford pupil to follow the music course. The resulting certificate, including an admirable pass in French, enabled him to gain admission to the University College of Wales at Aberystwyth.

While Irwyn Walters was a secondary-school pupil in Ammanford during wartime, successfully pioneering the study of School Certificate music, larger events were shaping his ultimate destiny. In 1916 and 1917 a Royal Commission, under Lord Haldane, examined the academic work of the fledgeling University of Wales. Among their main recommendations stood the notion that, through a more intensive study of music, and the involvement of all undergraduate students, a profitable connection between the university and the general cultural life of Wales might be fashioned. Dr W. H. Hadow, formerly associated with David Vaughan Thomas at Oxford, and, in 1917, principal of Armstrong College, Newcastle, was a member of the Welsh University Commission. Hadow was responsible for the musical recommendations, which were based on his experience of initiating extra-mural music courses among the working classes in the north of England. With Dr Thomas Jones of Rhymney, then deputy secretary to Lloyd George's War Cabinet, Hadow was able to appoint his protégé, Walford Davies, to two new posts in the University of Wales.

Walford had to be wooed from his comfortable, fashionable nest at the Temple Church in central London where he enjoyed a fully justified reputation as the greatest choir trainer of his day. Two factors worked the miracle. First, there was the magical sophistry of Thomas Jones, whom Walford was later to call 'the most wonderful man in the world, with the possible exception of another Welshman who was Prime Minister for Great Britain at the time' (H. C. Colles, *Walford Davies*, 118); second was the gold of endowment of a new Chair of Music at Aberystwyth by the two Davies sisters of Gregynog, which would offer Walford the financial blandishment he needed.

The role of the new Director of Music for Wales had been clearly set out in the Final Report of the Welsh University Commission in a passage written by Henry Hadow. The Commissioners declared that there was no people in Europe with whom song was a more intimate means of expression than the Welsh; but hitherto music had moved within narrow limits in Wales, and there had been little power of discrimination. The great choral societies did wonders with Handel and Mendelssohn, but, to a large number of Welsh people the whole literature of symphonic and concerted music was virtually a sealed book. Throughout most of Wales there was little or no chance of hearing *an orchestra* (see Ian Parrott, *Walford Davies*, 1942, 131). Forty years later in a BBC lecture, the composer Daniel Jones commented on this state of affairs: 'To the performer and to the composer, the song, the part song, the oratorio, were the whole of music; serious instrumental music, chamber music, symphonic music, extended musical forms other than oratorio – all these might have belonged to another planet.' (Daniel Jones, *Music in Wales*, 1961, 25.)

Walford Davies took up his new posts on 1 April 1919. That date also marked an epoch in the professional life of Irwyn Walters, and was the point from which the long march towards instrumental and orchestral expertise in Wales began. The promotion of instrumental capability started in a small-scale, practical way. Walford Davies wished to take real instances of good performance directly into schools and adult evening classes. So piano trios were created at Aberystwyth, Bangor (under E. T. Davies) and later Cardiff. Hundreds of concerts were given to elementary and secondary schools across the country. Usually Walford, from Aberystwyth, played the piano and delivered explanatory lectures, supported initially by the violinist Hubert Davies and the cellist Arthur Williams. These afternoon school performances might be followed by similar, more sophisticated concerts in the evening for adults. Much of the success of these widespread excursions depended on Walford's immense gifts as verbal communicator, which he developed on a larger scale in his remarkable talks on music for school pupils and for adults on the new BBC radio in the 1920s and 1930s.

Walford was nominally Irwyn's music professor at Aberystwyth. But it seems, from his recollections, that most of the substantial academic teaching at the university college was undertaken by Walford's deputy, the more modest and scholarly David de Lloyd. Even before he heard the performances of the College Trio, in Ammanford Irwyn had formed his own ensemble, with his brother Merfyn playing cello, and an old school-friend from Ammanford, Rae Jenkins (christened Horatio), on violin. Rae Jenkins was one of those extraordinary performers of this era (along with the cellist George Isaacs) who combined learning a stringed instrument with working as a collier. After the day shift, Jenkins (born 1903) not only played in local cinema bands, but also managed to obtain Associate and Licentiate diplomas of the College of Violinists, before eventually leaving Wales to study at the Royal Academy of Music, with support from subscriptions raised by the citizens of his native town. At the Academy he studied conducting with another inspirer of Welsh instrumental endeavour, Sir Henry Wood. Jenkins's conducting for the BBC Variety Orchestra associated him later with the comedian Tommy Handley, whose catch-phrase, 'Play-Rae', became a weekly feature of the wartime *ITMA* show on the radio. When he was appointed conductor of the BBC Welsh Orchestra in 1950, Rae Jenkins perhaps remembered the early encouragement he had received in Ammanford, and established a radio series entitled 'Students' Music Hour' in which youngsters intending to make music their career were given the opportunity of playing with a professional orchestra.

Rae Jenkins's and Merfyn Walters's string teacher in Ammanford was a local character and collier, George Evans. Such extraordinary figures were the idiosyncratic inspirers of many Welsh youngsters who went on to make substantial professional careers in English orchestras. In a number of Welsh townships teachers like George Evans banded their students together to form orchestras in the first half of this century. In Cardiff there were

Arthur Angle and Herbert Ware (in whose Junior Orchestra Alun Hoddinott enjoyed his first ensemble experience); Morgan Lloyd performed the same function in Swansea; Gomer Jones in Bridgend, and A. W. Bartholomew in Newport. There were also smaller groups of players inspired by people like Amos Harding, father of the string players Ronald and Kenneth Harding (the latter also a composer). Amos was remembered with affection and gratitude by Dorothy Adams-Jeremiah, first Music Adviser for Monmouthshire, as the chief encourager of her early musical endeavours.

In 1922 the National Eisteddfod visited Ammanford. In the light of contemporary remarks about the lack of orchestral experience in Wales, one might expect that Welsh instrumentalists would have suffered severe criticism. But the adjudicator of the orchestral competition at Ammanford, Sir Hugh Allen, Professor of Music at Oxford, expressed unqualified admiration. Six orchestras reached the final. Sir Hugh, with his co-adjudicator, W. H. Reed (leader of the LSO and Elgar's amanuensis for his violin concerto), standing beside him, delighted his audience: 'I said yesterday that you ought to have a Welsh Symphony Orchestra. You have already got it. (Cheers.) If you put two of the orchestras you have heard together, you would have as fine a band as anybody could wish to hear. (Applause.)' (See David Allsobrook, *Music for Wales*, 85.) The band which won at Ammanford was the Aberpennar Orchestra (Mountain Ash), conducted by remarkable local barber, Bumford Griffiths, who was later (with the Davies sisters' money) spirited away by Walford to gain a swift B.Mus. degree alongside Irwyn Walters at Aberystwyth. Griffiths was subsequently appointed orchestral co-ordinator under the Welsh Council of Music, initiated many string classes across south Wales, and established the massive Children's Music Festival in Cardiff in 1930, where string-orchestra performances by elementary-school pupils were at a premium.

The Ammanford judgement in 1922 was reinforced at the Pontypool Eisteddfod in 1924. There the first prize was won by Herbert Ware's Cardiff Orchestra, on an adjudication by Sir Richard Terry, the English musical scholar about to relinquish his post as Director of Music at Westminster Abbey. He was particularly intrigued by the high standard of performance among the solo wind and brass players. Those traditions in Wales had a considerable history, dating back to the Cyfarthfa Band, founded by Robert Crawshay of Merthyr Tydfil in 1847. The teacher of many of the 1924 Pontypool players was Sidney Tudor Roderick, bandmaster for the 3rd Battalion South Wales Borderers and of

Pontypool Military Band, also organist of St James's Church. Further evidence of growing expertise in instrumental playing was offered by the Draper family of Penarth. Charles Draper and his nephew Haydn became world-famous clarinetists, the latter playing in the London Wind Quintet alongside Leon Goossens and Aubrey Brain. All these elements were the raw material for the development of orchestral expertise and experience in Wales during the inter-war years.

Immediately after the First World War, Walford Davies became Gregynog Professor at the University College of Wales, Aberystwyth, and Irwyn Walters enrolled as an undergraduate, studying first French (to guarantee a secure career) and then music. The relatively young college, since its foundation in 1872, had a fitfully brilliant musical history. Dr Joseph Parry, rescued from obscurity in Dannville, Pennsylvania, became first Professor of Music in 1873; but his extra-mural activities – promoting both himself and the general cause of music throughout Wales – comprised one reason the impoverished college gave for his dismissal in 1879. In those six years, however, Parry had laid the foundations of a sound singing tradition among Aberystwyth students; and his former assistant, David Jenkins, later established the annual series of choral and orchestral concerts.

Another striking element in Aberystwyth's musical life before the arrival of Walford Davies was the endeavour of Mme Lucie Barbier, ex-student of the Paris Conservatoire and wife of the Professor of French. Independently of the Music Department, and holding no official position at the college, in 1910 she founded a music club which, for the next five years, presented concerts and recitals including an extraordinary range of contemporary European (and especially French) music, through performances by artists like Alfred Cortot and Raoul Vignes. Mme Barbier's efforts were aided financially by the Davies sisters of Plas Dinam. Indeed, she got as far as encouraging the sisters to sponsor the formation of a small orchestra in Aberystwyth which would give educational concerts throughout Wales. Her scheme also involved the appointment of 'foreigners' (Belgian and French) as instrumental teachers. After a quite promising start the Barbier–Davies music scheme collapsed, partly through the departure of leading teachers, partly due to a jingoistic wartime antipathy to foreigners of all kinds. And Mme Barbier's personal star plummeted when she deserted her husband and set up home with Alfred Zimmern, the brilliant new Professor of International Politics. Finally, in reaction to Aberystwyth puritanism, the couple migrated to Paris.

What Mme Barbier had proposed and set on foot during the war came to proper, steadier fruition after 1919 under Walford Davies. He was always fortunate in his aides and deputies: in the music lecturer David de Lloyd he could rely on those pedagogical and scholarly qualities which were needed to sustain the day-to-day life of the Music Department during the Professor's necessary and frequent absences. Hubert Davies, the violinist of the first Aberystwyth Trio, had been a pupil of Heifetz's teacher, Leopold Auer. Arthur Williams, the cellist, a native of Laugharne, had briefly been a member of the Joachim Quartet, and studied and worked in Germany, where he was interned as an alien for the duration of the Great War. It was through the Joachim connection that the great violinist's nieces, Adila Fachiri and Jelly d'Aranyi, began their association with music-making in Aberystwyth; and it was further due to them that their fellow-countryman, the young Bela Bartok, gave a recital of his own music at the college in 1922. The resident pianist, a native of Aberystwyth, was Charles Clements, an accompanist of brilliant accomplishment.

One of Walford's first objectives was to found a proper Aberystwyth Orchestra. He enlisted the help of members of Jack Edwards's Town Band, despite the perplexing disparity between 'orchestral' and 'band' pitches. As early as November 1919, Walford inaugurated the 'Students' Orchestral Festivals'. Music students had to attend all the rehearsals, whether they were instrumental players or not. Those who could play found themselves temporary members of the LSO, intimidated by the prowling Henry Wood, prince of orchestral disciplinarians. This was the post-war world of feverish musical activity into which Irwyn Walters was projected as an undergraduate. When he graduated in French in 1924 he was one of thirty-four such students; when he received his B.Mus. in 1926 there were four other graduands.

The 196th College Concert, on 6 March 1926, seems now almost a summation of Irwyn Walters's musical experience thus far. Two of his own songs were performed by Nellie Jones: 'Hiraeth', with string orchestral accompaniment conducted by David de Lloyd; and 'Y Sipsi', with Clements at the piano. A student choir, under Bumford Griffiths, sang madrigals; Dr David Vaughan Thomas gave a short talk on Schubert, then accompanied Evelyn Cook in Schubert's Sonatina in B flat. Finally, Schubert's Quintet was played by Evelyn Cook and W. H. Jenkins (violins), Kenneth Harding (viola), and Arthur Williams and Ronald Harding (cellos). From 1924 till 1926 Irwyn was deeply engaged in helping to organize the activities of the Music Club, whose visiting artists included the Dolmetsches and Leon Goossens. And he became

involved in the 'Director's Hour', a weekly session which the whole department had to attend, at which players played, singers sang, while work after work was studied and analysed. The year 1926 also saw the sixth annual Aberystwyth Festival, which was steadily building up experience of performances of classical orchestral and choral music under conductors like Elgar, Wood and the young Adrian Boult. Perhaps, as Ian Parrott has implied, Walford Davies was not the ideal inspirer of orchestral work: his real gifts lay in choral training. So, despite considerable advances in orchestral experience during his twenty years as director of the National Council, it was not until after the Second World War that an orchestral tradition was firmly established in Wales. It was, however, the buzzing musical activity generated by Walford Davies at Aberystwyth which prepared the ground and supplied many of the ideas which were to cohere in Irwyn Walters's formation of the NYOW in 1946.

In addition to those initial stirrings in Aberystwyth, Irwyn was surrounded after 1926 by the first signs of professional orchestral activity in Wales. Already, in 1920, a 'Welsh National Orchestra', created by T. Hopkin Evans with Walford's support, had briefly carried the torch through a pioneering series of concerts in south Wales towns. Then, in 1923, the National Council of Music

Aberystwyth music graduates, 1926, with tutors Sir Walford Davies (seated, centre) and (to his right) David de Lloyd. (Irwyn Walters, front row, extreme right.)

sponsored the Welsh Symphony Orchestra which, for several seasons, gave concerts throughout Wales, and performed at festivals and the National Eisteddfod under Boult, Wood and Walford Davies. Essentially the WSO had as its nuclei the university trios from Bangor and Aberystwyth, augmented at each venue by local teachers and semi-professional players.

In 1928 the BBC, combining with the National Council and Cardiff City Council (all with Sir John Reith's blessing), formed its first symphony orchestra in Cardiff. Under Warwick Braithwaite, and with Beecham, Elgar and Wood as guest conductors, it gave enterprising free lunchtime concerts to Cardiff office-workers in the awful acoustic conditions of the National Museum, and broadcast nationwide. Its repertoire even extended to Mahler's Fourth Symphony. This Welsh BBC Orchestra performed at the Llanelli Eisteddfod in 1929, but perished a year later through lack of funds. Nonetheless, that remarkable experiment must have heartened Welsh enthusiasts for orchestral performance, like young Irwyn Walters. The fully fledged BBC Symphony Orchestra, under Adrian Boult, was founded in London in 1930. For the past sixty years that supreme instrument has set the highest standards for all aspirant orchestral musicians. But it should be remembered that the first successful experiment on those lines had taken place between 1928 and 1930 in Wales.

Irwyn Walters's teaching career in its main outline during the ten years after 1926 reflected that of his influential teacher, David Vaughan Thomas: apprentice posts in English schools, followed by a return to the land of his ancestors. And like David Vaughan Thomas, who had chosen a wife, Morfydd, to be his implacable helpmeet through hard times, Irwyn in 1926 met his most dedicated partner and supporter, Margaret Jane Edwards. Denied suitable teaching opportunities in Wales, in 1927 he took up his first post as a junior-school master at Shebbear College, Bideford, where, in addition to music he taught general class subjects. He was responsible for class singing, some individual piano lessons, elementary violin teaching, and musical appreciation along lines pioneered by Walford, Stewart Macpherson, Ernest Read and Percy Scholes. Irwyn recalled that Shebbear College already had a comprehensive range of gramophone recordings, and that he used Walford's BBC broadcasts as part of his teaching method.

In 1928 he moved on to be the first music specialist at a London grammar school, Owen's School in Islington. There, one of his young pupils was the future BBC music producer, harpsichordist and musicologist, Lionel Salter, who was already being taught by the distinguished music educator, York Trotter. Salter remembers

Irwyn as a very young man with a shock of fair hair which stood straight up on his head. This is not a memory shared by those who knew him in early Youth Orchestra days, by which time he sported a very wide parting! Although Salter had been musically well taught before Irwyn went to Owen's School, the boy and the young man enjoyed the time they spent together preparing for the School Certificate Examination. Salter recalls Sir Percy Buck (who had been Vaughan Thomas's senior colleague at Harrow thirty years before) visiting Owen's School to inspect the work of the music department, and his being most impressed by Irwyn's efforts to develop instrumental music at the school.

There was another Welshman at Owen's School who was in charge of choral singing, already a distinctive feature of the school's activities. This master, Ben Morgan, was to become well known throughout Wales. Irwyn much later remembered him as '. . . an exceptional man, with a degree in Science, a Diploma in Art, and blessed with a light tenor voice. He performed in productions at the Old Vic, and sang several concert oratorios with London choral societies.' A report on music in schools in 1953 described Ben Morgan as '. . . a man with a kindly, cheerful personality . . . His way of persuading a class of children to participate spontaneously and joyfully in musical exercises, which until then were strange to them, was quite remarkable' (*Music in Schools*, HMSO, 1953). In 1936, Ben Morgan was to be instrumental in spiriting Irwyn back into the resurgent musical life of Walford's Wales.

While teaching at Owen's School, Irwyn married his Margaret on 11 April 1928 at Willesden. On 27 December their son Gareth, a future composer of distinction, was born. Irwyn became organist at Willesden Green Presbyterian Church, forming a choir which gave concert performances. In the following year, 1929, he took another important step in his teaching carer, moving to become the first full-time music master at King Edward VI School, Stafford.

The government report *The Education of the Adolescent* (1926), under the undoubted influence of the committee's chairman, Sir W. H. Hadow, had stressed the importance of music and the arts in the secondary curriculum. The headmaster of King Edward VI School, F. T. Nott, one of the more enlightened of his kind, was in tune with Hadow's aesthetic and educational doctrines, and responded accordingly. He wished to make his grammar school the centre of local musical activity. Irwyn was appointed first agent for managing this venture. His reply to the challenge thus offered him was to colour all his subsequent musical endeavours.

The chief stipulation thrown down by Nott was that the new

music master should develop *instrumental* music and form a school *orchestra*. There was already a preponderance of violinists among the pupils, so Irwyn acquired a cello and a bassoon and set about learning those instruments himself until he could enlist the teaching assistance of more advanced local exponents. He quickly founded an ensemble which he called the Stafford Strings. This group combined school pupils with amateurs. With these innovations he was following the current of recent developments in junior music-making in the West Midlands and elsewhere. In 1925 Ulric Brunner, headmaster of a school in Bridgnorth, had begun to plan a non-competitive schools music festival, along lines proposed much earlier by Walford Davies. The first such festival started successfully in 1927. In 1929 Mary Ibberson founded the Rural Music Schools Association to encourage musical culture in rural areas, and county music committees were formed to organize their music-making. It is interesting that while Irwyn was making his mark in Stafford, the bassoonist Archie Camden, later to become one of the early tutor-supporters of the NYOW, was establishing a children's orchestra in Manchester at the request of Walter Carroll, the inspired co-ordinator of musical activity among the city's pupils. One hundred and two violinists and two cellists applied for membership of Camden's junior orchestra; but there were no wind applicants. He light-heartedly suggested in his memoirs that a prejudice against wind players had existed since the twelfth century, when a Plantaganet law (like Mozart in the 1780s) had designated them 'rogues and vagabonds'. This shortage was certainly a general problem, even in the inter-war years. When Camden married for a second time in 1933, his mother-in-law complained that none of her friends had ever heard of the bassoon. She wished that her daughter had chosen a flute-player, or even a conductor!

At Stafford, Irwyn developed his conducting abilities. In 1922 he had attended the conducting course of Adrian Boult in Aberystwyth. And as a student he had travelled to London to observe at close hand the techniques of distinguished conductors of the LSO. In 1932 he produced a dramatic presentation of Coleridge Taylor's *Hiawatha* as the second half of a school concert, having participated in a similar performance at Aberystwyth in 1925. Here he was treading in the composer's footsteps, for the work had originally been commissioned for the North Staffordshire Triennial Music Festival and first performed at Hanley in 1899 under the composer's direction. Irwyn's performance was repeated in the Stafford Festival Week. The *Staffordshire Advertiser* reported that the choir of 350 voices 'responded readily to the conductor's baton'. The first half of the festival concert consisted of items by junior and senior school orchestras, in conscious imitation, perhaps, of the junior concerts which Walford had made a feature of the early Aberystwyth Festivals. The local newspaper further confirmed the impact Irwyn was making on musical activity:

> When, on one or two occasions, I had come across Mr Walters in action at Stafford, I became more than usually interested in his work. It seemed to me that he had just the qualifications for a good conductor. He is a Welshman, and therefore not short of divine fire, and he is a musician to his fingertips. At Stafford Grammar School, he has transformed the music of the school from a meagre 'side show' to an important and greatly valued feature of the school's work and life. His work at the Grammar School should bear good fruit in Stafford music in years to come . . . One could not help regretting that every big school in the country does not provide similar facilities in music making . . . It is . . . as a conductor that he has most impressed me with his possibilities – how far these possibilities may be realised, I do not pretend to prophesy, but I would like to see him get a bigger opportunity. (*Staffordshire Advertiser*, 1934)

Irwyn stayed at Stafford for seven very happy, active years. Throughout his stay in the West Midlands he retained contacts with his former colleague, Ben Morgan, and with Wales. One consequence was that he was engaged as an occasional inspector and lecturer under the Board of Education in Wales. With Ben Morgan he travelled through the principality giving lecture-recitals. They also adjudicated jointly at many music festivals throughout England and Wales. Finally, Ben Morgan persuaded Irwyn to apply for appointment as HMI for music in Wales. Although reluctant to sever his connections with Stafford, when his application was successful, he returned in 1936 to become the first full-time music HMI for Wales.

II   The Return of the Native

Irwyn Walters made Swansea the base for his new work as HMI in 1936. In this respect he was again imitating his old teacher, David Vaughan Thomas who, far from his beloved Swansea in 1934, had died in South Africa during one of his periodic tours as examiner for Trinity College, London. Irwyn's new official duties evidently did not preclude the pursuit of important music-making. Soon after his arrival he was invited to become honorary musical director of the Swansea Festival Orchestra; thus, it might be said, he was stepping directly into Vaughan Thomas's local musical shoes. The orchestra was a semi-professional body, currently experiencing some difficulties, which were soon resolved through their new conductor's capability as an administrator. It began its first series of concerts at the Brangwyn Hall in 1936, supported by an impressive list of 224 patrons.

This was no ordinary provincial venture. Part of the third concert of the third season was broadcast by the BBC on 31 January 1939. It included Beethoven's 'Prometheus' Overture, Handel's Eighth Oboe Concerto in B flat (soloist Leon Goosens), 'Il mio tesoro' sung by David Lloyd, and Dvořák's Fourth Symphony. 'Harmonicus', who had admired Irwyn's achievements in Stafford, wrote a review of the broadcast for the *Wolverhampton Express*:

> He is the conductor of the Swansea Festival Orchestra and a recent broadcast concert seems to have put the seal of success on his work with the orchestra during the past two years or so . . . The orchestra numbers over sixty players and all but a few are amateurs – miners, clerks, teachers, out-of-works, and so on. Stafford people and many others will be glad to hear of Mr Walters's success and will hope he may 'go farther' yet. (*Wolverhampton Express*, 13 February 1939)

A similar article in the *Daily Herald*, 1 February 1939, by Ronald Harding, Irwyn's fellow-student in Aberystwyth, suggested that Swansea, rather than Cardiff or Newport, was leading the way in stimulating a high quality of orchestral and choral performance. Irwyn was in overall control; but his guest conductors before the outbreak of war included Boult, Raybould (a future collaborator in the NYOW), Joseph Lewis and Boyd Neel. Among the soloists with the orchestra were Myra Hess (a close friend of Walford), Lisa Perli, Artur Schnabel, Leon Goossens, Ben Williams, Redvers Llewellyn and David Lloyd. The leadership of the orchestra alternated between Frank Thomas and Morgan Lloyd.

After the outbreak of war in 1939 the Festival Orchestra was disbanded. But this left a gulf which was eventually bridged by the formation, again under Irwyn's control, of a new band under the name 'Welsh Philharmonic Orchestra'. This ensemble gave ten concerts under Irwyn's direction between January 1941 and December 1942, with Morgan Lloyd as its first leader, then Garfield Phillips, and visiting soloists of the calibre of Clifford Curzon, Moiseiwitch, Cyril Smith, Florence Hooton, Eda Kersey and Peter Pears. One result of Pears's visit, as soloist in yet another performance of *Hiawatha's Wedding Feast*, was that Benjamin Britten's attention was drawn to the quality of the Pentrepoeth Boys' Choir which had participated in the concert with Peter Pears. Britten consequently chose that choir for the first public performance of his *Ceremony of Carols* and for the first recording of the work. In preparation for those events, Britten, Pears and Britten's Austrian amanuensis, Erwin Stein (father of Marian Thorpe) enjoyed truly Welsh hospitality at the Walters's family home. Also, Benjamin Britten took the opportunity of encouraging the creative musical ambitions of Irwyn's son, the fifteen-year-old Gareth Walters.

The special circumstances of wartime – London musicians had necessarily to be dispersed to the provinces, the BBC Orchestra to Bristol and Bedford, for instance – meant that Irwyn, as an HMI with wide-ranging musical contacts in Wales, became the most important agent for arranging concerts and recitals. He was engaged as conductor of the LSO for their visit to Swansea, 16 September 1943. His soloist in Rachmaninoff's Third Concerto was Moiseiwitch. Later the same year he took the LSO on a tour of Wales with the aim of (imitating Walford Davies and Ernest Read) introducing the best musical performers to audiences of children.

The first concert of the series was given in the Alhambra Cinema in Shotton on Deeside. Nearly one thousand children were assembled that afternoon. Senior pupils came from Deeside, Mold, Holywell and Flint. The programme included Mendelssohn's 'Hebrides' Overture, the Minuet and Trio from Haydn's Symphony No. 102. 'Moths and Butterflies' and 'The Wild Bear' from Elgar's *Wand of Youth* suite, and *Finlandia*. A local newspaper reported that the young audience's behaviour was 'marked by intelligence and intentness. Answers came with remarkable promptness to questions on music asked by Mr Irwyn Walters, who also conducted the orchestra' (*Chester Chronicle*, 3 June 1944). Similar concerts were given in south Wales. One of those has been vividly recalled by John Lawley Thomas, whose mother, Annie Lawley, had been accompanist to the great Ammanford Choir in Irwyn's youth. John, a pupil at Amman Valley County School (Irwyn's Alma Mater) was one of a party of schoolboys dragooned into attending an LSO concert.

> In 1943 the London Symphony Orchestra did a tour of south Wales. One afternoon at the end of school, lots of us joined the valley train to Glanaman. I went as a sceptic, persuaded to go by Miss Davies, teacher of Form IVB. We trooped into the Workmen's Hall, Garnant, which served as a cinema during the week. This building literally clung to the hillside, the floor of the gallery where I sat sloping at an alarming sixty degrees. Irwyn Walters conducted and explained the music, introducing some of the themes before the actual performance. *I remember the sheer ecstasy when the orchestra played*. I had never known such an experience . . . *I know it changed my life*, those catalytic moments with Irwyn Walters and the LSO. (Author's interview with John Lawley Thomas, 1988.)

Thirty thousand children heard Irwyn conducting the LSO during that 1943 tour. Rhoslyn Davies, the renowned Welsh conductor who died so tragically early, spoke on numerous occasions of the great impact the LSO's Rhondda concert had upon him.

Like earlier (though temporary) inspectors of school music in Wales – among them David Evans and David Vaughan Thomas – Irwyn Walters found that the status of music as a subject depended largely on the headmaster's notion of music's role, and also on the accidental expertise of individual teachers. Many small rural schools had no piano or no competent musician on the staff. But while Irwyn was pleased in the late 1930s by evidence of good choral singing in elementary and secondary schools, he was also encouraged by increasingly numerous signs of instrumental capability. For example, in the village school at Camrose, Pembrokeshire, he found that most of the pupils played recorders and read music-in-parts with confidence. Visiting Aberaeron Secondary School he found Rhiannon Daniel taking a class of forty boys, all playing recorders. She remembers his visit on a hot summer afternoon, when she mistook him for a workman as he stood casually leaning in a doorway, listening quietly. During his early years as HMI he was able to observe a rising standard of orchestral performance among secondary-school pupils at

Pwllheli, Gowerton, Neath, Merthyr Tydfil, the Haberdashers' Monmouth School for Girls, Llanelli and Aberdare.

Whitchurch High School, in the northern suburbs of Cardiff, and still today a centre of musical excellence, provides a striking example of how school music was developing during Irwyn's early years as HMI. The current (1995) head of music at the school, Anthony Josty, has recorded that when it had opened in 1937 there was no official music room. The music teacher, Leonard Manton, was one of ten general assistant teachers. The equipment for music lessons then consisted of a baby grand, a radiogram and a fine amplifying gramophone. A small orchestra of nine players performed under the direction of Mr Greenshields, head of physics, who also played the cello. The orchestra developed and thrived largely due to regular visits by three peripatetic teachers. There was a school music society which arranged recitals by distinguished artists. Irwyn Walters, as HMI, reported of Whitchurch High School in 1943:

> Music has played a vital part in the corporate life of the School since it opened . . . The Music master has laid the foundations of a fine musical tradition here, and this has already spread far beyond the immediate school environs. Music now stands as a firm bond of friendship between the School, the Parents, and the local community.

Exactly the same judgement might be made of Whitchurch High School fifty years later, under Tony Josty and Eric Phillips.

It might further be said of Irwyn Walters that the early period of his HMI career until 1946 was, in one respect, frustrating. He still wished to be a teacher and communicator, rather than simply an inspector and reporter. Mrs Gaynor Howard, recently retired as head of music at Howell's School for Girls, Llandaf, remembers an inspection by Irwyn Walters at her first school:

> In 1956, during my last term at Abergavenny High School [for girls], Irwyn Walters was the HMI for Music who visited the School during its General Inspection. It was my first post: I had been there three years, and it was my first meeting with Irwyn Walters. Having heard so much about him in connection with the National Youth Orchestra of Wales, I imagined a towering figure, and was therefore surprised to find him short, spare and balding. But what riveted me was that piercing gaze! Contrary to all my fears, he found the department (which was run single-handed, and included individual lessons, class violin and cello lessons, as well as the usual round of class music), running smoothly. He

was delighted to find an embryo orchestra and a small choir. I remember so well his eagle eye examining books and yet asking very few questions, *itching to take over a class and demonstrating his instant rapport with young people.* (Author's interview with Gaynor Howard, 1989.)

III   Founding an Orchestra

Stewart Macpherson, the renowned pioneer of music education, founded the Music Teachers' Association in 1908. One of its chief aims was to develop skills of musical appreciation in the population at large. The secretary was Stanley Harper, an employee of Boosey and Hawkes, in whose Regent Street premises the association had its headquarters. Harper had organized summer courses for young orchestral players in London before the Second World War. As the end of hostilities approached he began to think about reviving those meetings. Wartime conditions in London made it impossible to hold courses there; and so the idea of a residential course in the countryside was born.

In January 1943 the Music Teachers' Association held a meeting at the Royal Academy of Music to discuss the possibility of organizing a residential summer school orchestral course for young musicians that year. Irwyn Walters's interest in promoting orchestral studies in schools was well known, and so he was invited to attend. The record of that meeting shows that it comprised 'many well-known music masters and mistresses in schools as well as representatives of Education Authorities'. Leslie Regan, the association's chairman, presided, supported by Ernest Read (one of the initiators of the youth orchestra movement), Mme Elsie Horne, Mr Forbes-Milne, Alec Rowley, Tracy Robson (representing MTA members) and Cyril Winn, HM Chief Inspector of Music for Schools. An advisory council for the course was formed from 'distinguished members of the music-teaching profession and those interested in education. The meeting closed with a definite mandate to the MTA to proceed on the lines discussed' (minutes of the meeting, January 1943). The proposed course was part of a sequence of such meetings for young orchestral players which had been begun by the MTA under Ernest Read's direction since the late 1920s. The prospect of a new course, scheduled for 1944, aroused widespread interest, and records show that 563 applications were received for 210 places.

Irwyn Walters was delegated to approach directors of education in Wales for their support. He was also made responsible for carefully choosing the limited quota of secondary-school pupils from Wales, the cost of whose participation would be borne from local-authority funds. Eventually Sherborne School for Girls in Dorset was chosen as the venue for the course which would last from 21 to 28 August 1944. Its director was Ernest Read. A film record of the course, which has since unfortunately disappeared, was made by the British Council for the purpose of spreading information abroad about British cultural activities. On reaching Sherborne the players were re-auditioned for allocation to orchestras A and B. All the Welsh candidates, with one exception, were admitted to the premier ensemble, Orchestra A.

Such was the shortage of wind players in the schools of Wales at this time that the first Welsh contingent at Sherborne consisted solely of string players. In choosing them Irwyn was able to turn to a few reliable centres where he knew solid pioneering work was in full flow. Sir George Dyson, principal of the Royal College of Music, had spoken of those individuals in Wales who, before the general advent of local music advisers, did so much to muster musical forces in their areas. These local leaders, approached by Irwyn Walters, were W. H. J. Jenkins in Pwllheli, Cynwyd Watkins in Gowerton, Harold Lews in Milford Haven, Gwilym Ambrose in Aberdare, Arthur Giardelli in Merthyr Tydfil, Frances Rees in Cardiff and Isobel Cook in Monmouth.

The 1944 Sherborne course was so successful that it was repeated in the following year. In 1945 the Welsh players included a clarinetist from Monmouthshire, a pupil at Pontypool Girls' County School. This was the daughter of the local bandmaster, P. Baden Bowen, who on his own account had won the woodwind solo at the 1924 Pontypool Eisteddfod, when his performance had encouraged Sir Richard Terry to express great optimism about the future of Welsh instrumental playing.

Such were the main events which immediately preceded the founding of the National Youth Orchestra in 1946. However, in a recently published and, in places, startlingly inaccurate book, Dr Ruth Railton, founder of the National Youth Orchestra of Great Britain in 1948, has told a markedly different tale. In an attempt to establish the significance of her undoubtedly splendid orchestra Dr Railton has been guilty of large sins of omission and a measure of distortion. She claims that her attempt to start what she initially called the 'National School for Young Musicians' was repeatedly sabotaged in the immediate post-war years by the musical establishment in England, led by the very same Music Teachers' Association which had started the Sherborne venture. A former conducting pupil of Henry Wood, working independently, and lacking any firm financial backing, she claims to have approached

Dr Sydney Northcote, Music Director of the Carnegie Trust, for advice and moral and financial support. Earlier, Cyril Winn, Chief HMI for Music, while admiring her enthusiasm, had warned her 'of the barriers for a young person trying to start something, especially a woman'. That meeting with Winn took place in May 1945, in other words almost a full year after the first very successful Sherborne course, which Dr Railton refers to by name not at all. Her claim that she was attempting something new in 1945 is without substance. Her later meeting with Northcote took place, ironically, on 1 March 1946, when he told her that he had been unable to gather the financial backing which she required and, Railton claims, he had promised.

In a most extraordinary passage, Dr Railton recounts personal events which took place in 1948, two years after the Sherborne meeting, and a year after she visited the second course of the National Youth Orchestra of Wales in Caerleon:

> After a short August holiday we returned to work with renewed vigour, only to discover that the summer conferences of various teaching and musical organisations had been discussing our plans, and now most, on the instructions of Sydney Northcote, regretted that 'on education grounds' they would have to withdraw their support . . . musical education should remain in the hands of the established guardians thereof. The latter seemed to be the Music Teachers' Association and the Schools Music Association. *At this time there were various summer schools for amateurs, students and teachers* . . . (R. Railton, *Daring to Excel: The Story of the National Youth Orchestra of Great Britain*, 11–24, our emphasis.)

The casual dismissal of earlier successful efforts, implied in the final sentence above, requires that the record should be set straight. Railton's refusal even to mention the long-established educational efforts of Ernest Read in the orchestral field merits a firm rebuttal. It can also be argued that the members of the MTA were probably quite justified in their scepticism towards the efforts of a relatively untried young freelance musician, particularly since what she proposed seems an unnecessary replication of the successful Sherborne venture without visible means of official support.

The pressure from Welsh schools for representation at the Sherborne course became so great that it far exceeded the permitted quota of pupils from Wales allowed to take part; Irwyn Walters decided that the only solution was to make separate provision at home. And so in the second half of 1945 he began exploring the possibility of inaugurating a wholly Welsh venture. To achieve this he had to solicit help from every director of education in Wales, apparently a marathon task. In fairness, however, he would not have to encounter the difficulties bitterly recalled by Ruth Railton in England; Irwyn Walters already carried with him his authority as a widely respected HMI, with long-established musical contacts throughout Wales and in the wider world of professional music; and Wales possessed a far more clearly etched educational homogeneity than England, enjoying the co-ordinating influence of the Central Welsh Board (soon to be replaced by the Welsh Joint Education Committee in 1951) and the Welsh section of the new Ministry of Education. But he also had to find a venue for the first Welsh course. Finally he was able, thanks to the help, sympathy and understanding of Miss McDonald, headmistress of Haberdashers' Monmouth School for Girls, to accommodate the orchestra at that school for its first meeting.

Since the first venue for the National Youth Orchestra was to be Monmouth, administration of the course was generously undertaken by Monmouthshire Education Authority under the enlightened guidance of Charles Gittins, one of the great Welsh directors of education, and later to be a distinguished professor of education in Swansea. He delegated the main task of administration to his clerk, Mr Westram. Gittins also had the support of a very capable county music organizer, Mrs Dorothy Adams-Jeremiah, a native of Abertillery who had once been a piano pupil of Amos Harding, father of Ronald and Kenneth. She had subsequently trained as a singer at Cardiff University and the Royal College in London. Irwyn Walters became Director of Studies and was responsible for auditioning prospective members. The criterion for membership was that each candidate should be of Welsh extraction or resident in Wales. Local education authorities were to cover the expenses of the participants.

The task of auditioning prospective members was most demanding. In 1945 few counties had music advisers. Merioneth had appointed the first, John Hughes, in 1942, and other counties followed towards the end of the war. The majority of the players Irwyn recruited were from the more densely populated industrial areas in south Wales where private tuition was more easily accessible. There were numerous violinists, but no viola players, so certain violinists were persuaded to move to the viola to make up that section. The majority of brass players were members of local brass bands who received tuition from their seniors in the band, or their fathers. One such boy was Harold Nash from Merthyr Tydfil, a gifted young trombonist who was later to become a professional player. Several other brass players came from the Ammanford Silver

The pioneers of the NYOW, left to right: Irwyn Walters, Ronald Harding (string tutor), Clarence Raybould, Mrs Dorothy Adams-Jeremiah (Music Advisor for Monmouthshire), Archie Camden (wind tutor), Mr Westram (clerk to Charles Gittins).

Band: Derek James (trombone), Glanville Jones (bass trombone) who was already a miner, and Lyn Evans (horn). Irwyn recalled waiting to audition Glanville Jones as he came straight from working in the pit at Cross Hands in Carmarthenshire. Glanville later gave up mining to play in the Covent Garden Orchestra.

Finding woodwind players was more difficult in the early years, and initially the orchestra had to rely on English students recommended mainly by Archie Camden. He provided two of his bassoon pupils, Brian Pollard and Alan Way. The first principal oboist was Janet Craxton who came at the direct request of her father, the distinguished pianist and musicologist Harold Craxton. Other players in subsequent years included Dinah Demuth, daughter of the composer Norman Demuth, and she later became principal oboe in the City of Birmingham Orchestra. But by 1950 the Welsh Orchestra had become self-sufficient in native players of minority instruments.

Irwyn needed to select the first conductor of his young orchestra with great care. He required someone possessed of a natural affinity with young people and who was also sufficiently well known to claim public support. He therefore decided to approach Clarence Raybould who he knew was soon to retire as assistant conductor of the BBC Symphony Orchestra, and who had been a collaborator in Irwyn's Swansea Festival ventures before the war. Clarence Raybould later described their significant meeting:

One day in the autumn of 1945, while rehearsing the BBC Symphony Orchestra at the People's Palace in the Mile End Road,

I was always fortunate in my early career in being able to take part in collective music-making – in orchestras and chamber music groups. Around 1936 I was a member of the Herbert Ware Junior Orchestra at Cardiff, and throughout my school days at Gowerton Grammar School – 1939–46 – the inspired activities of C. K. Watkins ensured a high level of performance in orchestral, chamber and choral music. Indeed the music-making at Gowerton must have been unique in Wales at that time.

However, none of this really prepared me for the overwhelming experience of playing in a large orchestra that could reach a professional standard in both its technical achievement and its wide-ranging repertoire. And in Clarence Raybould, the first conductor of the National Youth Orchestra of Wales, we had a highly sophisticated musician of great depth and temperament with a degree of past achievement and international standing that I certainly had not previously encountered. It was possible for the first time in Wales to come into close contact with and experience this storehouse of knowledge and professional guidance – and here it is perhaps appropriate to mention that not only was Raybould a conductor who had premièred many foreign works of note in this country and a pianist of remarkable sensitivity and accomplishment, but also a composer whose early opera *The Sumida River* had been produced as far back as 1916.

One outward sign of his wide-ranging sympathies was his enthusiasm for the music written by Welsh composers, and their works featured regularly in his programmes – a tradition that has survived to the present day. Little did I think then that at a future date I would experience the thrill of hearing the orchestra play some of my music.

As a young musician who was beginning to explore seriously the creative side of music-making I was more than grateful for the time and patience that 'Clarry' lavished on my early efforts and was very much influenced and guided by his critical and detailed comments. And as a practical musician the benefits gained by playing in this orchestra under Raybould's baton and being rehearsed and taught by some of the most distinguished and respected performers of the day were incalculable and proved to be of lasting value and importance.

Alun Hoddinott

I was told that Mr Irwyn Walters, one of HM Inspectors for Music in Wales, wished to see me. He had come from Swansea to lay before me a scheme he had been dreaming of for some time for the establishment of a Youth Course in Orchestra Playing for school children in Wales. The idea appealed to me very much and in the next summer holidays, I went down to Monmouth School for Girls to begin work with a body of young people chosen from the schools in Wales . . . so a scheme started which was destined to bring into being the National Youth Orchestra of Wales, the first of its kind in Europe, possibly in the world! (Interview with Clarence Raybould reported in *Radio Times* on the occasion of the Youth Orchestra's televised broadcast on BBC Concert Hour, 1956.)

IV   The First Ten Years

It is well worth reiterating, at this point, the remarkable fact that the National Youth Orchestra of Wales was the first of its kind in the world, by nomenclature and function. It seems hardly likely that in 1946, Miss McDonald, headmistress of Haberdashers' Monmouth School for Girls and temporary hostess of the orchestra, anticipated how original the venture was, much less that it would be sustained for at least forty more years. She had originally expected to share her school in the summer holiday with her young Scottish nephews. In addition she found the school invaded by seventy-five lively young musicians. The two nephews were delighted. Nine-year old Allan made friends with bassoonist Alan Way from Glasgow; Allan's daughter Katarina was in fact taught the bassoon much later by Alan Way. The other nephew, Ian Forsyth, fourteen years old, had brought his bagpipes with him, but was quite happy to sit and listen during orchestra rehearsals.

In addition to Clarence Raybould there were two other course tutors. Ronald Harding, who had been at Aberystwyth with Irwyn, took charge of strings. He had just relinquished his position as principal cellist with the LPO to become Director of Music for East Sussex. World-famous bassoonist and versatile musician Archie Camden was in charge of wind players. His mother had been and accomplished pianist, while his father was a flautist who showed a keen interest in many other orchestral instruments. Camden took oboe lessons with Charles Reynolds, principal in the Hallé Orchestra, who some years later was to teach Leon Goossens. Camden, who also played trumpet, double bass and timpani, had evidently absorbed his father's wide-ranging instrumental interests, and had been taught piano by his mother. In 1904 at the age of sixteen he attended the Royal Manchester College of Music for bassoon tuition with Otto Schieder, principal in the Hallé Orchestra; though Camden found himself the only bassoonist in the college orchestra. He was also a member of Walter Carroll's class in harmony and counterpoint. Subsequently he was principal bassoon in the Hallé and Liverpool Philharmonic orchestras; and much later he enjoyed the distinction of playing the Poulenc Trio with the composer at the piano.

Clarence Raybould receiving
an enthusiastic welcome
from orchestra members.

The ages of the seventy-five players who assembled on 25 July 1946 ranged between fourteen and twenty years. Many of them had never before performed in a symphony orchestra or experienced boarding-school life. The leader was Leonard James, a sixteen-year-old schoolboy, winner of twenty-two prizes at National Eisteddfodau. The wind section consisted of two bassoons, two oboes, two clarinets, two flutes, three French horns, three trumpets and three trombones. The work schedule was very demanding. It consisted of a three-hour rehearsal of the full orchestra in the morning under its conductor Clarence Raybould, sectional rehearsals in the afternoon, and a full rehearsal again in the evening. On the Sunday evening of this first course an impromptu concert was given for the young players by Ronald Harding on cello, Archie Camden on bassoon, accompanied by Clarence Raybould on piano, who earned Camden's complete respect as a pianist: 'Clarence was superb, a really first-class pianist. It was not only technically perfect, but had all the feeling, the nuances and sensitivity of a top-line chamber music player . . .

What an example for many pianists'. (Interview with the author, 1989.)

The wind section at the first orchestra course.

Gareth Walters, Irwyn's son, was a participant in this first venture which he has called 'that historic course'. He remembers that his father asked him to fill the only remaining vacancy in the orchestra, on timpani. This somewhat worried Gareth in prospect: it was the age before pedal-tuned timps, and he thought he would be unable to hear the notes, gently tapped with the middle finger, with all the other noise going on around him. He recalled (in a letter to the author, 1989): 'Help came from an unlikely source, the bassoonist Archie Camden, whose job was to coach wind and brass. Surprisingly he was also experienced in percussion matters too, and a few short but intensive lessons with him soon convinced me that the problem was not insurmountable.' He also retains images of the Monmouth School Hall, which had not seemed big enough to contain a large gathering of teenagers with all their impedimenta. There were also 'the tennis courts where we spent much of our spare time: and the warmth of the sun (was every summer *really* long and hot in those far-off days?) reflected from the grassy banks in front of the school.'

Another participant, the clarinetist Betty Connah (née Bowen) who had been a member of the 1945 Sherbourne course, retains

It was the end of July 1946, and with my harp strapped to the wall of the guard's van I made my way by train from north Wales to Monmouth. I was met at Monmouth Junction, with kind foresight and a small truck, by Irwyn Walters and my harp was carefully trundled along to Monmouth Girls' School.

No doubt I felt somewhat superior on this first National Youth Orchestra Course, for had I not already studied one whole year at the Royal Academy of Music, played in the First Orchestra under Clarence Raybould and in the Second Orchestra under Ernest Read, while most of my new colleagues were still at school? Mind you, while I was a pupil from 1939–45 at Denbigh County School the only symphony orchestra that I had ever seen was the Liverpool Philharmonic conducted by (then) Dr Malcolm Sargent at the Pavilion in Rhyl.

I had met Irwyn Walters while I was at school, perhaps when he was an Inspector of Schools, and I have a clear recollection of him attending a service at my chapel when I was officiating at the organ – I had been playing the organ in church since I was twelve years of age.

Curiously, my recollections of the Monmouth course are still vivid: *The Walk to the Paradise Garden* by Delius, with its lush, sensuous harmonies, and the grotesque *Danse Macabre* by Saints-Saëns. In the latter I had to start the piece by tolling midnight on my harp; the orchestra roared with laughter when Clarence Raybould at rehearsal accused me – unfairly, I thought – of playing thirteen chimes. For this piece Saint-Saëns calls upon the leader to tune down his top E string to E flat to add to the macabre nature of the music. When we came to play the public concert at the end of the week our leader could not find the E flat and Clarence Raybould indicated that I should sound my E flat for him. Such were the tensions of our 'first night' – he had not encountered any difficulty previously. I remember also Dvořák's Eighth Symphony in G (we knew it then as number 3 – his symphonies were later renumbered); there was no harp in this, but I enjoyed its fine melodies and I still recall the exciting trombone playing of Harold Nash.

Ah yes: it was there that I met a pretty young lady from Pwllheli – she was our principal viola player; we were to meet again a year later at the RAM, and we have been meeting ever since. Then she was Rene Ellis Jones, but from January 1951 she became known as Rene Ellis Ellis. No wonder my recollections of the Monmouth Course of 1946 remain quite vivid.

Osian Ellis

very clear memories of Monmouth: 'I remember my mother working out how many "coupons" I would need to cover the food ration during my stay.' In those early days Betty Connah was the only Welsh woodwind player, and, in addition to friendships formed with imported English players, she recalls lasting relationships fashioned at Monmouth: for instance, Nancy Sweet, flautist, later married Pat Strevens, principal horn. Both became

My father knew Irwyn Walters since the beginning of time, or so it seemed to me. He was a regular visitor at the garage with his car for servicing, but that was something my father and he discussed only in passing. The proper topic for the day would be music. And so it came to pass that the idea of a Welsh 'children's' orchestra came alive in 1946. I remember listening with considerable trepidation to the two of them discussing whether I was perhaps too young to go away without Mami for the first time. What a relief when they decided to take the risk. Even if I was still wearing short trousers, I was fourteen! The final decision was taken because there were seven of us from Ammanford in the orchestra.

So came the great day, 26 July 1946. I had had strict orders to keep track of what I spent, so I kept a little notebook, which I still have. It cost 2*s*.8*d*. for a bus ticket from Neath, then 11*s*.11*d*. for a train to Newport followed by a 1*s*.3*d*. bus ticket to Monmouth. Then there was the long climb up the hill to the school. Boy, were we glad to get there.

On the first Sunday, the string section met Mr Ronald Harding, someone who was to change all our ideas about what we could do. It was my, and I dare say everyone else's, first personal contact with musical genius. No one else in my entire musical life has ever had the same effect on me, including all my teachers at the Royal Academy in later years. To say that he terrified the section into playing way beyond the sum of our individual capabilities is an understatement. We were mesmerized, but we learned fast or suffered a tongue-lashing in front of everyone. After the dust settled the strings gave out a sound that would not have been a total disgrace in professional circles.

Those who remember Ronald Harding's 'every note a pearl' and other words of wisdom will appreciate an episode which took place in Swansea Training College about 1948 (Glamorgan was playing the West Indies at St Helens and Parkhouse made 88 before skying a catch to Worrell at mid-off – yes we did get some free time!) during a string rehearsal of Elgar's *Sospiri*. It was a *very* hot day and things were getting pretty tense. The *Sospiri* starts marked *ppp*, and from then on it's downhill all the way. Mr Harding wanted it quieter so it was, 'one hair of the bow'. Not quiet enough. So we went to 'one inch of the bow'. No good, and by now he was changing colour in total rage at our inability to play a proper *ppp* to please him. So it came to 'one inch of one hair', this for a note tied across goodness knows how many bars. 'Why can't you play really quietly?' came the enraged question. Again, '*Don't move the bows*'. Nobody did, and then came the commendation 'Perfect!' Total silence followed, and then a sheep outside said 'Baaaaaaa'. But no one dared laugh until Mr Harding did. The tension broke, but we sure did learn to play *very* quietly. Such was the lot of the strings: we survived and were the better for it.

Arwyn Jones

professional musicians. She, too, cherishes the memory of Archie Camden: 'How hard he worked with us! He never raised his voice but achieved satisfying results with gentle persuasion.' Clarence Raybould carried a white handkerchief in his trouser pocket 'which he extracted with a flourish whenever he needed to attract

MONMOUTHSHIRE EDUCATION AUTHORITY.

Souvenir Programme.

NATIONAL YOUTH ORCHESTRA COURSE

MUSIC DIRECTOR:

CLARENCE RAYBOULD.

FINAL CONCERT

ROLLS HALL, MONMOUTH—AUG. 1st, 1946.

OVERTURE	...	Prometheus	...	Beethoven
MARCH	...	Wand of Youth (No. 2)	...	Elgar
INTERMEZZO		Walk to the Paradise Garden	...	Delius
SERENADE FOR STRINGS (First Movement)			...	Mozart
DANSE MACABRE	..	...	...	Saint-Saëns
SYMPHONY No. 4 in G.	...	...	...	Dvorak

(Movements 2 and 1).

A souvenir programme of the final concert given at the first orchestra course.

the attention of orchestral members whose eyes were fixed too closely on their music copies.' Betty Connah until recently taught at Haberdashers' Monmouth School for Girls where over a hundred pupils are currently learning wind instruments. (Letter to the author from Betty Connah, 1989.)

At the conclusion of the course the orchestra gave a delightful and varied programme to an appreciative audience in the Rolls Hall, Monmouth, many of whom were parents of orchestral members. A local newspaper commented, 'Monmouthshire Education Committee and Mr Irwyn Walters are to be congratulated on this bold step to further the course of British music.'

The course which made the greatest impact on me was my first – 1947. The excitement was intense. We were meeting instrumentalists from every part of Wales and some, because of the dearth of bassoon players in particular, from outside. Four schools were prominent: Neath, Pwllheli, Llanelli and Gowerton. In all four music flourished because of the dedication of their music teachers. Among the Gowerton contingent were Alun Hoddinott and Haydn Davies (who was to succeed Irwyn Walters as HMI), while from among the Llanelli contingent was Michael Evans who was to become a distinguished chamber-music cellist. Then there were the heavy brass, as Clarence Raybould called them, the trumpets and trombones – Reg Potter, Brian Buckley, Harold Nash and Graham Peel. Of the members from over the border the two girls from the Royal College of Music, Wendy Robinson and Deirdre Dundas-Grant, were exceptionally good bassoon players. But for me the star of the orchestra was Bill James (or Leonard James as his name appeared on programmes). His playing was a revelation, particularly in the solo variation in the Suite in G by Tchaikovsky.

The course took place at Caerleon Training College (as it was then) and it came as a shock to see the next day's porridge being laid out in bowls at six o'clock the previous evening. But there were more shocks to follow. When we got down to work we quickly realized that we were no longer the stars of a small school orchestra. 'Every note a pearl', 'one hair of the bow' and 'only an inch of bow' were to become the new language: none of us who sat under the glare of Ronald Harding has forgotten his mesmeric control. After his sectional rehearsals one would slink upstairs to practise and reach those positions which had 'never been reached before'. We poor bass players were using borrowed school instruments, some with strings which had a greater affinity with telegraph wires. Norman Mason from Pwllheli was the only one with his own instrument and was a full-time student at Manchester. The rest of us in his section had to rely on occasional help from amateurs.

The full rehearsals taken by Clarence Raybould were often accompanied by amusing repartee, particularly between Raybould and fourth horn Donald Roberts. To have a conductor from the BBC Symphony Orchestra instructing us and treating us as serious players was entirely new. The wind rehearsals taken by Archie Camden, the world-famous bassoonist, were also entertaining and instructive. With Ronald Harding, the cellist, they showed us the professional approach to music-making. Intonation had to be secure, rhythms had to be precise and the commitment had to be total. This attitude changed all of us into being better musicians. Yet, all this did not happen by any accident or decree. It was due to the vision and persistent efforts of one man who eventually managed to persuade one local education authority to house and administer the project. This was, of course, Irwyn Walters. He, single-handed, recruited the members by visiting schools, bands and youth centres and then acted as Director of Studies during the courses. Without his dream we would all have been the poorer.

John Glynne Evans ('Jingles')

Granville Jones, the first
soloist to appear with
NYOW, 1947.

In 1947 the Welsh National Youth Orchestra Course was held at Caerleon Training College in Monmouthshire. There were seventy-five members, exactly as before, and Leonard James remained leader. The youngest member was twelve-year-old Michael Jenkins, whose father was the W. H. J. Jenkins who had been responsible for much of the pioneering instrumental work in north Wales and was by this time music lecturer at the Llandrindod Wells Emergency Training College. Michael was already versatile enough to help out as either violinist or violist in his father's orchestra, as required. Ammanford, Merthyr and the Rhondda provided many of the brass players, from their strong local brass traditions. For the first time a soloist was engaged, in the person of violinist Granville Jones from Cymmer. Having completed National Service he was studying at the Royal Academy of Music. He had been nominated by the vice-principal of the Academy after giving a brilliant performance of the Elgar Violin Concerto with the Academy orchestra under Raybould.

Even at this early stage the new orchestra was attracting international attention. During his conducting tours, for instance, Clarence Raybould had been questioned in Scandinavia, Yugoslavia and the Netherlands about his association with this startling new venture. More significantly, perhaps, Ruth Railton, who had been working for CEMA (Committee for the Encouragement of Music and the Arts), expressed an interest in the Welsh venture. So Irwyn Walters invited her to the Caerleon course in 1947 to observe the orchestra in action. She left Caerleon, it seems, brimming with enthusiasm and confirmed in her desire to carry out her own plans. Yet when it came to writing about her own orchestra – in a book more than 400 pages long – Dr Railton chose to omit even the briefest reference to the National Youth Orchestra of Wales. Her only comments on this visit to Wales combine blind disparagement with cutting chauvinism. Of a later auditioning tour of Wales for her embryo orchestra she tells us that, 'in March 1948 instrumental work in Wales was at an early stage, and in Cardiff there was more promising playing than natural talent', though she thought Swansea to have more potential, 'with a rugged native bite, more personality, more eagerness'. Of north Wales she said, 'the Welsh sing, of course, but instrumental work was not strong.' And local teachers aroused her paranoia: 'In the smaller places the MTA was at work, as people said to me, "I hear you are going to exploit the young to fill your own pocket."' The latter imputation was as wildly wrong-headed as her opinions on Welsh musicality were ignorant. (See R. Railton, *Daring to Excel*, pp.35, 39–40.)

The orchestra gave two concerts in 1947, in Newport and Swansea, and Raybould declared that the standard of playing had improved since the previous year. At Caerleon Training College in 1948 there were eighty-five players in all, with four in each wind and brass section, though still only two bassoons. For the first time Wales supplied two of the oboists.

The year 1948 was marked by the orchestra's first appearance at the National Eisteddfod of Wales. Irwyn Walters had been invited by the music committee of the Eisteddfod to join its board of judges. He replied that he felt he could make a more valuable contribution to the events of Eisteddfod week by bringing the National Youth Orchestra to play at the concert on Youth and Children's Day. In previous years this concert had consisted solely of choral items by winning groups, and a pageant. Irwyn suggested that the NYOW should be responsible for half the items in the concert, and his proposal was readily accepted by the music committee who also agreed to pay any expenses incurred by the orchestra. Irwyn also insisted that Clarence Raybould should remain conductor.

The combined choral and orchestral concert took place on 2 August and was a resounding success. The *Times* commented, on 5 August,

A youth orchestra recruited from players up to the age of eighteen from all parts of the Principality played under Mr Clarence Raybould and gave so good an account of itself that it raised hopes of dispelling that indifference in Wales to any but vocal music for which Sir Walford Davies strove so arduously and apparently unsuccessfully.

That sentiment was echoed by the *South Wales Evening Post*:

Why should Wales remain in the nineteenth century? Her resources are now happily very different. She need no longer confine herself to part-song. She can now partake of great music which is as much part of her heritage as any other nation. Why should she pursue the beggarly life of a songstress now that her Youth Orchestra can perform a Brandenburg Concerto and a Dvořák Symphony?

The wind section of the orchestra received particular praise from the *Liverpool Evening Post*:

The brass were especially good throughout, and it is difficult to

Clarence Raybould and the string section led by Bill James, 1949.

find a weak spot in the ensemble. Much of the woodwind is carried by young women players and they never faltered. Surely this is the most significant event that has occurred in Welsh music in the past quarter of a century.

Interviewed for *Reynolds News*, a national Sunday paper, Clarence Raybould said that whilst conducting in Finland he had spoken with Sibelius, who expressed an anxious wish to hear the Youth Orchestra performing one of his own works. At the National Eisteddfod in Bridgend, BBC engineers recorded a concert which included Sibelius's *King Christian* suite for a future broadcast, and so it would be possible for the great man to fulfil his wish. (The composer was actually present at a concert given at Easter, 1950, when that work was repeated. He was eighty-two years old at the time, and the author vividly recalls the distinguished, white-haired gentleman sitting in the audience.)

In 1949 the orchestra tackled its most ambitious programme so far. The National Eisteddfod was to take place in Dolgellau, where the organizer of musical events would be John Hughes, the first Welsh county music adviser, and elder brother of Arwel Hughes,

I was thirteen when the Glamorgan Education Authority began organizing Youth Orchestra courses, first at Dyffryn House, and later at the School Camp, Ogmore-by-Sea, where my mother's cousin, Islwyn Williams, the well-known short-story writer, was Director of Studies. Here was my first experience of real music-making. The same summer, I got into the National Youth Orchestra of Wales, and being very much the baby of the course was completely spoilt by Mrs Adams-Jeremiah, then Monmouthshire's Music Organizer, and by Mr Irwyn Walters, the HMI due to whose vision the Welsh Youth Orchestra courses had been started, and without whose inspired organization they would not have continued. 'Clarry' Raybould, whom I personally adored, was the conductor, and our harp tutor was Maria Korchinska, on whom I modelled myself – aristocratic Russian bearing and all – for some years afterwards. It was a marvellous experience. I began to live for the Youth Orchestra courses, and I was very proud to be one of the select few chosen from all over Wales for its National Youth Orchestra. Irwyn Walters aroused all our nationalistic zeal – we would have considered it treason to even apply to go to the rival organization, the National Youth Orchestra of Great Britain.

Ann Griffiths,
in Meic Stephens (ed.) *Artists in Wales*, 1977.

distinguished composer and musical administrator. John Hughes was widely known as an excellent choral conductor and took charge of the choir of 600 children who were to perform two groups of songs at the Youth and Children's concert. He asked Irwyn Walters if he could persuade Clarence Raybould to provide orchestral accompaniment for a group of songs taken from Gluck's *Orpheus* and conduct the work himself. Raybould readily agreed. It was also decided to combine the Eisteddfod visit with the Orchestra's first tour of north Wales.

Numbers had by now increased to 101. Caerleon College was again the base of rehearsals, and the tour began with a Newport concert, 21 July, followed by a civic reception. Selwyn Jones, the correspondent of *Reynolds News*, was careful to point out that most of the initial support for the orchestra had been provided by the Monmouthshire Education Authority, despite some people still denying that the county was truly a part of Wales. Monmouthshire was in fact responsible for all the early administration of the NYOW from 1946 to 1951, through the good offices of Mr Gittins.

One of the concert pieces of 1949 was Dvořák's *Slavonic Rhapsody* No. 3 in A flat, in which there are passages for harp. It was decided to give parts to three harpists, Ann Griffiths, Mair Jones and Lydia Richards. Ann Griffiths, now a distinguished professional harpist and musicologist, had been introduced to

Maria Korchinska, harp tutor, with Ann Griffiths and Margaret Humphries.

orchestral playing in Russell Sheppard's pioneering summer orchestral camps at Ogmore-by-Sea in Glamorgan. At the age of thirteen she became a member of the NYOW, 'very much the baby of the course'.

Meanwhile it was reported in the *Western Mail* that Irwyn Walters had been asked to contribute to a White Paper on Wales a piece entitled 'The significance of the National Youth Orchestra'. At this time he was receiving considerable encouragement and support from his colleague, Dr William Thomas, Chief Inspector of Schools for Wales. Also in 1949, tentative suggestions were made for the orchestra to appear at the Llangollen International Eisteddfod the following year and at the 1951 Festival of Britain. Clearly, then, in the short space of four years, the NYOW had 'arrived' as an important element on the British musical scene.

In 1950 numbers had increased to 110. Two residential courses were held, the first at Easter in Rhoose Emergency Training College, where there were two soloists, Olwen Davies a soprano from Swansea, and Gwyn Griffiths a baritone from Caerphilly. The summer course was again at Caerleon, and as the National Eisteddfod was at Caerphilly, Irwyn was invited by the music committee to arrange another combined choral and orchestral concert. The organizers wished to replace Raybould with a conductor of their choice, but Irwyn adamantly supported his own man. The orchestra shared the evening with a choir of 800 children trained by Russell Sheppard, and in the instrumental part of the programme they played Arwel Hughes's *Fantasia* in A minor for strings.

Their summer tour consisted of twelve concerts. On their visit to Aberystwyth Clarence Raybould was unable to appear, but Archie Camden made an excellent deputy. The principal of University of Wales College, Aberystwyth, Ifor L. Evans, presided at the evening concert and said how pleased the college was to act as host to the young players. He might well have signalled the event as a belated fulfilment of the orchestral promise engendered in the college thirty years before by Walford Davies. The Haverfordwest concert was not well attended, and a local newspaper reporter deplored the local lack of enthusiasm for all forms of artistic endeavour, while taking comfort in the thought that an inspiration was being provided for the youth of Wales in the field of music.

The pride of the orchestra was hurt – and truth travestied – by the appearance of an article in an illustrated weekly paper in the summer of 1950. It claimed that Ruth Railton's recently formed National Youth Orchestra of Great Britain was 'the only thing of its kind'. Most indignant of all was Clarence Raybould who, after flying back from the USA to conduct his Welsh musicians, said, 'I must apologise for my countrymen, because, if I may say so, there is nothing in the world quite like the Welsh National Youth Orchestra, and I am prouder of it now than ever' (*Illustrated Weekly*, 1953). This was one of the numerous instances of the failure to understand how original Irwyn Walters's conception had been.

The next year, 1951, was Festival of Britain Year, and for the first time the orchestra was led by a young woman, Leila Palmer from Solva in Pembrokeshire, a nineteen-year-old student in her second year at the Royal Academy, and her third as member of the NYOW. She showed great presence of mind in a concert at the National Eisteddfod in Llanrwst: when the soloist, Granville Jones, had the misfortune to break two strings, she handed him her violin and the performance continued. The orchestra, now 114 players, was accommodated in Bangor Normal College, and the concert tour of mid and north Wales contributed to the Festival celebrations in each town visited. Ronald Harding remained as string tutor, while Charles Farncombe replaced Archie Camden in charge of wind. Camden eventually took the considerable experience gained in Wales to assist in training the National Youth Orchestra of Great Britain in 1954. Dr Railton provides an interesting little footnote to his career, without ever mentioning his prior time with the NYOW: she remarks, 'I had always wanted the famous Archie Camden in my team, but earlier he had links with the MTA [Music Teachers' Association], so I didn't approach him' (Railton, *Daring to Excel*, p.176).

In 1951 all the players' names were printed in the concert programme for the first time. Every area of Wales was represented, though there were only seventeen from the north. Nominations were submitted by local education authorities who paid £14 towards the attendance costs of any student in their areas. Selection was handled by Irwyn Walters who travelled all over Wales auditioning prospective members, going to great lengths to hear everyone who applied. Geoffrey Francis, latterly Music Adviser for Mid Glamorgan, recalls Irwyn Walters visiting his home to audition him; and Vernon Bailey-Wood speaks of his second audition in Porth County School after failing to gain admission a year earlier: 'I was amazed to find that despite the many people he must have auditioned, he still remembered my previous unsuccessful effort.' He was accepted, and the arrival of the envelope containing the course music still remains in his memory. 'The only item I can recall was a brand new copy of Smetana's 'From Bohemia's Woods and Fields' in a bright orange Goodwin and Tabb folder. It was almost totally illegible and looked as though it had been printed with a large potato.' Vernon Bailey-Wood tells how the standards among the string players were maintained:

Rehearsals with Clarence Raybould were generally pretty relaxed, but string rehearsals with Ronald Harding, normally a charming man, were sometimes a nightmare. Playing desk by desk or even on one's own was absolutely mortifying. Occasionally Irwyn would watch from the side-lines and from time to time there would be a tap on the shoulder and somebody would be moved up or down through the desks of strings. This was pretty nerve-racking. (Letter to the author, 1989.)

New members of the orchestra spent their first year as probationers, and were only retained for a second year if they had made satisfactory progress. Each student who attained the required standard was awarded a certificate of membership signed by Irwyn Walters and Clarence Raybould, and given a membership badge. The upper age-limit was set at twenty years, which meant that the composition of the orchestra was continually changing, and that promising talent received the chance to develop.

When the Welsh Joint Education Committee took over the administration in 1952 only four of the original orchestra members

NYOW, 1952 (the year the WJEC took over the administration of the orchestra).

remained. The transition took place quite smoothly, so that many members were unaware that administrative change had occurred. But there were noticeable changes in personnel. The secretary of the WJEC, Wyn Jones, and his assistant, Miss Brooks, came in place of Mrs Adams-Jeremiah; the cellist James Whitehead replaced Ronald Harding as string tutor, and Norman Fawcett succeeded Charles Farncombe. Some local authorities were by this time thinking of running their own orchestras. Monmouthshire was one of the first, Dorothy Adams-Jeremiah enlisting the help of Ronald Harding as conductor. Russell Sheppard had already begun similar distinguished work in Glamorgan. During the next ten years most Welsh local education authorities organized their own county courses, thus enabling many more children to participate in orchestral music-making.

The leader of the NYOW in 1952 was John Davies from Brynmawr, and the soloists Maureen Thomas and Olwen Williams (piano), and Patricia Kern, later to become a distinguished contralto. The course was held in two centres, Llandrindod Wells and Cardiff. The National Eisteddfod was at Aberystwyth, and there Clarence Raybould was invested a member of the Gorsedd of Bards in recognition of his contribution to the Eisteddfod and the musical life of Wales. The orchestra now numbered 120, and on 7 August part of the concert programme was recorded by the BBC for transmission on *Children's Hour*, prefaced by an introductory talk on its short history from Clarence Raybould.

The wind section, 1952.

In 1953, by invitation of the General Overseas Service of the BBC, the orchestra contributed to a special Coronation series of programmes entitled *Commonwealth Concert Hall*. Other participating orchestras were the combined ensembles of Sydney and Melbourne, the New Zealand Broadcasting Symphony Orchestra, the symphony orchestras of Toronto and Montreal, Cape Town and Johannesburg, the Scottish National Orchestra, the Hallé Orchestra and the Royal Philharmonic Orchestra. The Welsh orchestra's programme was broadcast worldwide in association with Queen Elizabeth's visit to Wales in July, 1953. The NYOW also recorded for the BBC the signature tune, 'Leading Through', for a broadcast series *Leslie Bailey's Log Book* relayed in the autumn and winter of 1953.

The summer course took place from 24 July to 10 August, first in Wrexham, then in Swansea. The joint leaders were Cecily Holliday and Hilary Squires, with Arwyn Jones as sub-leader. Harold Nash, a former member currently playing in the Sadler's Wells Orchestra, was appointed brass tutor. The fifth consecutive annual concert was given at the National Eisteddfod, and on this occasion the orchestra made its first television appearance from the Pavillion at Rhyl. The programme included a movement, Allegro Scherzando, from Welsh composer Daniel Jones's Symphony No. 2. The author recalls the difficulties experienced by many members in reading this work from the manuscript score. The soloists at the concert were Joan

The cello section (Haverfordwest, 7 August 1954).

Davies (soprano) and Eifion Williams (clarinet). By now, only two of the original members remained: Hilary Squires (violin) and Haydn Davies (French horn).

In 1954 the course was held in Swansea and the soloists were Eira West (piano) and Joan Davies (soprano). The programme included Elgar's complex Introduction and Allegro Op. 47, for String Quartet and String Orchestra. The members of the quartet were Stuart Shelley and Denise Bassett (violins), Pamela Lewis (viola) and Geraint John (cello). A report by Kenneth Holland on the Ystradgynlais National Eisteddfod reflected the difficulties the orchestra experienced on one of the hottest evenings of the year. He described the Elgar performance as 'rather shaky', and judged that Brahms' Second Symphony was nearly calamitous. He also criticized Joan Davies, describing her performance as 'emotionally underweight'. Another reporter's comments on the Swansea concert were more favourable, awarding particular praise for the performance of Massenet's ballet music from *Le Cid*: 'Here was something ready-made for a young and enthusiastic orchestra . . . hitherto restrained young wind instrumentalists blew with undisguised relish, though enthusiasm in general never outran control' (*South Wales Gazette*, 1954). Excerpts from the programme were again recorded by the BBC for future radio transmission. Later the same year the University of Wales conferred on Clarence Raybould the honorary degree of Doctor of Music for his services to Welsh music.

NYOW, Edinburgh International Festival 1955.

In 1954 the National Youth Orchestra of Great Britain had been invited to play at the Edinburgh International Festival. Irwyn Walters decided to approach the Artistic Director, Ian Hunter, about the possibility of the NYOW being given the same opportunity. Hunter asked to hear BBC recordings of the orchestra in his London office, and was so impressed that he immediately invited them to play. It was stipulated that the orchestra for Edinburgh should number no more than 100, and that the programme time be limited. With the prestigious booking in the bag, Irwyn drove straight away to Barry to invite the Welsh composer Grace Williams to write a work specially for perform-ance in Edinburgh on 3 September. She readily agreed, and 'Penillion' received its first performance at the Usher Hall.

In the year of the NYOW's Edinburgh Festival concert, special arrangements were made for preparatory training. In addition to the customary summer course, held at Caerleon and Bangor, there was a special short course in Wrexham in late August and early September for those members of the orchestra who would be selected to perform in Edinburgh. In the larger course there were 131 players. James Whitehead had three assistants for the strings: Cecily Holliday and Mary Diddams (both ex-members of the orchestra), and Ernest Haigh, principal double bass with the BBC Welsh Orchestra. Colin Davis, some time before entering on a distinguished career as conductor, replaced Norman Fawcett as woodwind tutor, and Harold Greensmith took the place of Alan Bixter. The leader this year was Julian Shelley from Rhyl, and the soloist Frederick Davies (bass-baritone).

Joan Davies joined the orchestra in Caerleon as she was to sing

45

Although I was the only candidate from Porth County School, Irwyn Walters found time, in the spring of 1952, as he had the year before, to come to the school to audition me for the NYOW. I was amazed to discover that despite the many people he must have auditioned he still remembered my previous unsuccessful effort. Eventually the envelope of course music arrived. The only item I can recall was a brand-new copy of Smetana's 'From Bohemia's Woods and Fields' in a bright orange Goodwin and Tabb folder. It was almost totally illegible and looked as though it had been printed with a large potato.

I suffered growing apprehension as the steam train chugged towards Llandrindod Wells, and once there everybody seemed so good – 'What the hell was I doing here?' Rehearsals with Clarence Raybould were generally pretty relaxed, but string sectionals with Robert Harding, normally a charming man, were sometimes a nightmare. Playing desk by desk or even on one's own was absolutely mortifying. Occasionally Irwyn would watch intently from the side-lines and from time to time there would be a tap on the shoulder and somebody would be moved up or down through the desks of strings. This was pretty nerve-racking.

The year 1955 could be regarded as the moment the orchestra arrived. We were invited to play at the Edinburgh Festival. A slimmed-down version of the orchestra spent a week at Wrexham before travelling north. We stayed in a camp at East Linton a few miles east of the capital – a rather spartan establishment.

Edinburgh was very impressive – ascent of the Scott Memorial was mandatory for all members of the orchestra. The Usher Hall itself was rather unprepossessing from the outside. I have a photograph of two juxtaposed advertisements outside the Hall, one announcing a concert by the Philharmonic Symphony Orchestra of New York, the other shared between us and the Scottish National Orchestra.

The concert was televised – live, I think. This was quite an event in those days. My parents watched it on the set of some 'rich' neighbours. Frankly I can't remember much about the concert itself, though I recall that there was some concern about the wearing of white and the glare of highly polished brass instruments. I do, however, remember being accosted by a wildly enthusiastic American who was astonished that so many marvellous young players could be gathered from such a little place as Wales.

On our return home a number of us in the Rhondda contingent talked our way on to the pantechnicon of Griff Fender, who had the contract for moving the heavy equipment. So I spent my twenty-first birthday and ended my happy association with the NYOW in the back of a furniture van.

Vernon Bailey-Wood

with them in Edinburgh. After the Newport concert Kenneth Loveland described this year's NYOW as 'the best that has so far been assembled'. He went on, 'the Orchestra has an added quality; there is about the performance a unity of outlook, a sense of inner purpose which one looks for only in the established symphony orchestras of long tradition' (*Western Mail*, 1955). He noted that the orchestra had never been so strong in its sectional leaders.

At the special course in Wrexham in August it was decided to forsake the summer dresses usually worn by the girls, in favour of something more formal. The dress adviser was Beti Davies, and the girls were to wear blue dresses with a cream bib, the boys grey trousers with cream shirt and maroon tie. On 1 September staff and students travelled to West Linton near Edinburgh to prepare for the Usher Hall performance. They were accompanied by representatives of the WJEC and the Welsh Secondary Schools Association. The Permanent Secretary and Chief Inspector of the Welsh Department of the Ministry of Education were also in the party. A courtesy visit was paid to the Lord Provost on the morning of 3 September, the day of the concert.

The Usher Hall concert was an outstanding success, Neville Cardus, the famous *Guardian* critic, wrote:

> Not once did the critical listener have to make allowances. If the orchestra had been heard behind closed doors by someone unaware that young people were making music, he might have hesitated to say whether this or that professional orchestra were in action.

The National Youth Orchestra of Great Britain had played at the festival a year before, and so it was only natural that comparisons should be made, even if, when applied to young players, they might seem invidious. A local newspaper critic wrote, 'The impression persists that the National Youth Orchestra of Wales played with more vigour . . . The crown must be awarded to the Welsh players for their lovely singing tone.'

V Promise Fulfilled: The End of the Beginning

On the tenth anniversary of the NYOW in 1956, a long-playing record was produced to commemorate the occasion. This was of a performance of Dvořák's 'New World' Symphony, and had been recorded by Douglas Rosser, a recording engineer for Qualiton Records, when the orchestra had played at the Usher Hall in 1955. A reception was held at the Park Hotel in Cardiff to launch the record. Its colourful sleeve contained the story of the growth of the orchestra in notes written by Kenneth Loveland, editor of the *South Wales Argus*. The reception was attended by three well-known Welsh composers, Mansel Thomas, Daniel Jones and Alun Hoddinott. The recording summed up all the remarkable things that had been achieved since Walford Davies had initially tried to stimulate instrumental music-making in Wales in 1919. In 1956, too, Irwyn Walters was awarded the OBE for his services to music in Wales, and in particular for his initiative in founding the NYOW, probably the greatest Welsh orchestral achievement thus far.

Daniel Jones wrote his overture *Ieuenctid* as a tenth-birthday gift for the NYOW and it was performed during this year's tour. The first part of the course, held in Llandrindod Wells, boasted 134 members, and of those 117 proceeded to Swansea Training College for the second phase. Julian Shelley again led the orchestra, and the soloists were Lorna Ellis (soprano) and Michael Evans (cello).

While they were rehearsing in Sophia Gardens Pavilion for the Cardiff concert, which was to be televised, a Dutch visitor to Wales, Mr Van Welzenis, was sitting at the back of the hall listening. Impressed with what he heard, he approached Irwyn Walters during a tea-break to invite the orchestra to play in Holland. The afternoon concert in Sophia Gardens, shown on *Concert Hour* at three o'clock, was introduced by Daniel Jones. When the orchestra performed in Swansea they were given a special tenth-birthday tea. Students of Cardiff Catering College had baked a cake weighing 112 lbs which stood 9 inches high, and was decorated with two harps and the orchestral badge. The ten candles were held in daffodil sconces with lettering in Welsh. The Mayor of Swansea entertained a party of 150, including the

Irwyn Walters, with Mrs Margaret Walters and their son Gareth, pictured after receiving his OBE award in 1956.

orchestral staff. Irwyn was called upon to blow out the candles.

A total of 151 players assembled in Bangor for the first part of this year's summer course. The new leader was Denise Bassett and the soloist Gerwyn Morgan (bass). By this time, of the ten orchestral staff, most assistant tutors were former members of the orchestra. David Wynne specially composed a *Fantasia for Orchestra* based on the folk tune 'Y Gwcw Fach' to be performed on this tour. Kenneth Loveland was reported in the *Western Mail* as judging the 1957 orchestra as 'the best . . . which has so far been brought together', suggesting that a probable reason was the retention for three years of several of the principals, thus creating continuity of leadership in several departments.

Mr Van Welzenis had confirmed his invitation to Holland in a letter to Irwyn in January 1957. The Welsh LEAs generously guaranteed to pay the fares of the 100 select players who would participate in this first foreign venture. After completing tours of both north and south Wales, culminating in a final performance at the Brangwyn Hall, Swansea, the selected 100 players boarded a train for the continent. The organization of the visit had been a complex affair. Nowadays foreign touring is accepted as a relatively normal part of youth orchestra, choir and band activities; but in those days it was a novel and unusual event. The 1957 tour was described by Anthony Randall, then a NYOW member, now well known as horn-player and conductor, as 'a fantastic opportunity'. Part of the transport problem was solved by the Rotterdam Symphony Orchestra who generously loaned double basses and timpani to the NYOW, and the main travel and accommodation arrangements were handled by the Dutch tourist organization, Prisma.

The party was divided into groups of twelve for the journey, each with a housemaster, housemistress and nurse. Clarence Raybould, generally an accomplished linguist, was the only member of the party able to speak Dutch, since he had been the first foreign conductor to visit Holland after the Liberation. The *Musical Times*, in October 1945, reported that he had visited Amsterdam to conduct the world-famous Concertgebouw Orchestra whose even more celebrated conductor, Willem Mengelberg, was then in exiled disgrace, having collaborated enthusiastically with the Nazis during the war. Members of the WJEC travelled with the NYOW, among them Wyn Jones,

It is amazing to think that some thirty-five years ago Irwyn Walters saw potential in my very raw, untutored horn playing when I auditioned for the National Youth Orchestra of Wales. His incredible perception, boundless energy, and the great pleasure derived from giving his players the opportunity to express themselves under the expert musical guidance of Dr Clarence Raybould, were a joy to behold.

I will never forget the trip to Holland as principal horn, playing great music such as the César Franck Symphony to incredulous audiences; the opportunity to play six concerts throughout Wales, and a BBC TV performance as soloist in Strauss's First Horn Concerto. Then came several fulfilling years as horn tutor until Clarence Raybould retired.

There are many like myself, from working-class backgrounds, performing music all over the world with great orchestras, who owe everything to Irwyn Walters's encouragement and that all-important first opportunity.

I remember when my parents, supportive as ever, arrived at the Brangwyn Hall for my last concert as principal horn. Irwyn greeted them: 'We have a marvellous horn section so I have chosen Brahms' First Symphony so that they can shine'. And shine we did!

Surely it is time that Irwyn was accorded the recognition he so richly deserves for his unique contribution to instrumental music in Wales by founding and running the first National Youth Orchestra.

Anthony Randall

---

secretary to the WJEC. They crossed the Channel overnight on a Dutch boat. The cellist Helena Braithwaite (née Davies), sometime music adviser for South Glamorgan, and sister of a former member, the horn-player and cellist Haydn Davies, recalls the journey:

The Channel crossing was very rough and I found it impossible to sleep. The larger instruments were stacked for the journey in a cabin at deck level, and I became increasingly concerned about my cello, having visions of it being washed overboard and floating on the high seas. I decided to go to reassure myself of its safety only to find the cabin where the instruments had been stored was empty. But my immediate panic was short-lived when I discovered that the instruments had been transferred to another cabin where they were strapped to the bunks for safety. (Letter to the author.)

Some of the orchestra members, during the rough $6\frac{1}{2}$ hour voyage, soothed the other passengers with choral singing. They travelled from the Hook of Holland to Rotterdam Central Station, where there was an official welcome. Then, in small groups, they were

Julian Shelley (leader) and fellow orchestra members at the Edinburgh Festival.

despatched to their host families. Helena Davies, leader of the cellos, and Denise Bassett had to share a room. On the first night they could not find the bed and slept on the floor. On the second night they discovered that the double bed folded down from the wall.

Thursday was set aside for rehearsal, though Dutch sound engineers arrived to make recordings, and the resulting programme was broadcast later that evening, including interviews with Clarence Raybould and James Whitehead, and orchestral members Kenneth George (principal flute) from Neath, and Gwenda Lewis (clarinet) from Aberystwyth. On Friday they travelled to Nijmegen by coach to give their first live public concert. Here the warmth of the welcome was partly due to local memories of the Welsh soldiers who had fought alongside the Dutch during the Liberation. Two concerts were given at the Riviera Hall in Rotterdam, situated in the Zoological Gardens. The Hall was surrounded by living exhibits in glass cases, and the audience sat, eating, drinking and chatting while the orchestra played, which some players found strange and distracting. But there was an enthusiastic ovation at the end. The last concert took place in the glass-making town of Leerdam, and the orchestra went on a conducted tour of the glass factory, each member receiving the gift of a cut-glass bowl.

Kenneth Loveland summed up their continental achievement in a broadcast on the Welsh Home Service, 25 August 1957. He said that the tour had been more than musically successful: it had been a 'diplomatic and ambassadorial success as well'. The young players had lived with their Dutch hosts and learned much of their ways, cementing lasting friendships.

> The tour has indeed been the supreme justification of the care which has been taken to organize this orchestra, a tribute to the work of Irwyn Walters, the Director of Studies, and a compliment to the foresight of the Welsh Joint Education Committee whose administration makes the renewal of this orchestra possible each year.

The NYOW had indeed reached a peak of achievement in 1957. Loveland further attributed its success to the partnership of Irwyn, behind the scenes, and Clarence Raybould working in the public eye. The administrative role of the WJEC was generous and smoothly managed. It therefore seems most regrettable that so successful an undertaking as the Dutch tour, leaving a glow of achievement which everyone enjoyed, should apparently have masked underlying signs of dissension.

On 7 September 1957, very soon after the orchestra's return, H. Wyn Jones, secretary of the WJEC, received a letter dated several days earlier from Dr Raybould stating that, in his view, it was essential for the future well-being of the orchestra that its organization and administration be radically revised. He had regretfully come to the conclusion that he could no longer continue as conductor under existing arrangements. He was invited to meet the chairman of the WJEC, H. R. Thomas, the chairman of the local authorities sub-committee, Llewellyn Heycock, and H. Wyn Jones on 19 September in Cardiff to discuss the matter. There was a further meeting of the four men in London on 10 October when the situation was thoroughly reviewed and tentative plans for a revised scheme were discussed. On the 21 October, in Cardiff, a third meeting took place, involving H. R. Thomas, Alderman Heycock, William Evans and H. Wyn Jones. Wynne Lloyd, chief inspector of the Welsh Department of the Ministry of Education, and Irwyn Walters HMI were invited to attend. Lloyd and Walters were presented with a scheme for their approval; they were in no position to object. Subsequently Dr Raybould was appointed to the joint posts of Conductor and Musical Adviser to the WJEC on matters connected with the orchestra, thus effectively taking over all Irwyn Walters's duties.

This striking change, and the callousness it represented, aroused a great deal of well-informed indignation. The general public were perhaps unaware of the important part played by the unobtrusive

An informal group with Clarence Raybould (centre) B. G. Griffiths (right) and James Whitehead (string tutor).

man who had originally conceived of the orchestra – the first such body in the world – and brought his plans to fruition by dedication and hard work. Only those who had been intimately involved in the work of the NYOW knew how much Irwyn Walters had done for the young people of Wales and the considerable help he had given in promoting young musicians in professional careers. Clarence Raybould had received all the public plaudits; and well he deserved them. But it is as well to remember now that Irwyn had possessed the visionary good sense to appoint Raybould in the first place.

James Whitehead, tutor and assistant conductor to the NYOW, was so indignant on hearing of the proposed change that he resigned immediately. In a letter written from Zurich to the editor of the *Evening Post* he described the dismissal of Irwyn under the scheme as 'unwarranted and inhuman'. Grace Williams, whose 'Penillion' the orchestra had played at their Edinburgh Festival Concert in 1955, disagreed with the suggestion that the change was essential for the future expansion of the NYOW. She wrote to the *Evening Post*,

> I can't see that the change has been made in the interests of further expansion. I can't see that Mr Walters can in any way be a stumbling block to any kind of expansion . . . He has done wonderful work and it seems inhuman that he should be taken away from what he has created.

53

One report went so far as to suggest that the administration of the orchestra had suffered by a clash of artistic personalities which necessitated such changes; but this explanation was neither confirmed nor denied by the parties involved. Irwyn Walters's abiding concern remained for the well-being of the orchestra he had created, and although he must have been deeply wounded when told that he was no longer required, his professional integrity as an educational civil servant caused him to withdraw quietly without making public or personal comment.

He did, however, make one significant formal gesture of resignation, in the shape of brief letters sent to every Welsh secondary school with which he had made professional contact, and to every current member of the Youth Orchestra. To the latter he wrote on 21 February 1958,

> You will know that my association with you all has been brought abruptly to a close. You may also have heard that our good friend Mr James Whitehead no longer feels able to serve the organisation. He and I are very sad to leave you all but shall cherish the happiest memories of our companionship together.

The youngsters responded in droves, and their letters are a most touching blend of affection, bewilderment, regret and intense gratitude. Irwyn Walters had been their musical 'father', had known many of their parents, and was perceived as a demanding encourager of their epoch-making endeavours.

Jeffrey Lloyd wrote to Irwyn,

> Last year the Orchestra was probably at its peak. This achievement, however, the culmination of ten years' hard work and perseverance, would not have been possible without the inspiration of the Orchestra's founder, [who] saw it develop from the embryonic stage into that of a musical team . . . The Orchestra will certainly miss the persons of yourself and Mr Whitehead. [I] thank you most sincerely for giving me the opportunity of joining your orchestra, thereby giving me a good start in what I hope will be a successful career.

Myra Thomas wrote, from a training college in Saffron Walden, about her distress on hearing the news, 'I am sure all the older members of your Orchestra feel deeply about this. We all respected you and knew that if there was any trouble we could talk to you, that you would understand and act for the best, always to our

Grace Williams

advantage.' Her teacher, the cellist and headteacher Harold Lewis, initial guide of so many NYO members, wrote to Irwyn from his primary school in Hakin, Milford Haven, 'I should be only too pleased to support you in any way possible. Already your ears will have been burning on several occasions when I have let go my wrath on "officialdom".' The Hubberston Symphony Orchestra, of which Harold Lewis was director, sent a formal typewritten complaint to the WJEC about Irwyn's treatment. Headmasters and headmistresses across the whole of Wales delivered notes of regret, protest and gratitude, since they, of course, had known Irwyn as encourager in his HMI guise, as well as in his complementary function as selector of instrumental talent from their schools.

It will never be perfectly clear what were the circumstances which led to his dismissal. In the correspondence there are fleeting clues relating to sharp, casually spoken words which may have been taken as insults during the Dutch tour. But the cause may have run deeper and longer than that; and the composer Grace Williams, in the course of an extensive, sympathetic letter to Irwyn, might well have identified the motives of those politicians within the WJEC who decided so perfunctorily to 'dump' him:

> I thought you might like to know that CR [Clarence Raybould] wrote a very affable letter to me and asked if I had anything to offer for this year's NYOW season. I wrote back and said that after the way you had been treated I had no wish to associate myself with him or the WJEC this year or any other year – though I was sorry to have to forego the pleasure of meeting and working with the Orchestra . . . I don't know the nature of his complaints or accusations, and I am not concerned with them, because I have seen you at work with the Orchestra and always thought your way of dealing with the youngsters was just right in every way – and it was obvious to everyone that they had a great respect for you.

Whether Grace Williams was well informed or not, it has been an unfortunate recurring feature of Welsh cultural and political life over the past hundred years that the promise of great achievement has often been dashed by teacup storms of interpersonal rivalry, destroying the greater good of all by petty indulgence in envy, jealousy and in-fighting. Irwyn Walters was an unforeseen casualty of political machinations. It is therefore even more to his credit that the magnificent instrument he had created survived the crisis of 1957 in the long term and remains in 1995 a monument to his unselfish endeavours. The recollections of its members recorded here alone reinforce the widespread feelings of deep

respect and affection in which the memory of Irwyn is still held by all who benefited from his vision and commitment.

Nevertheless, despite the associated bitterness, Irwyn Walters's dismissal in 1957 permitted him to deploy his undiminished enthusiasm, skills and experience on a wider stage. Soon after his departure from the NYOW he was busy founding the Franco-Welsh Orchestra, with the assistance of directors of French *conservatoires* of music, spreading abroad the Welsh gospel of the youth orchestra. After all, as he might well have acknowledged, it had been in Europe that the first stirrings of interest in international co-operation for young music-making had taken place. This had happened in most unpropitious circumstances. Jeunesses Musicales is an international movement which began in Belgium in 1940 to spread the practice of living music and related arts in schools and universities. From the beginning it dissociated itself from any doctrinaire political affiliations, and its influence spread to France in 1941 through the work of René Nicoly. A later aim of Jeunesses Musicales was to arrange for international co-operation among young orchestral musicians, and it was constituted part of the Federation Internationale des Jeunesses Musicales in 1945. By 1976 thirty-five countries across the world were linked to the FIJM.

The first meeting of Irwyn's new orchestra took place at Aix-les-

The European Youth Orchestra (soloist Margaret Price).

Four of the most interesting and rewarding holidays which I have ever enjoyed were spent playing with L'Orchestre Franco-Galloise in France during the summers of 1959–62. The orchestra comprised certain players from the National Youth Orchestra of Wales and others from Paris Conservatoire and other French music schools. The first concert in 1959 was played in an open-air auditorium at Aix-les-Bains (constructed, appropriately enough, at the expense of William Ewart Gladstone!).

My most vivid memory was of our first meeting with fellow wind players from Paris who greeted us with some reserve – doubtless feeling that no Welsh player could possibly match the standard of the Conservatoire. After a few minutes of rehearsal time they were astonished at the ability of the Welsh players to read at sight (and well-nigh perfectly) any music set before them. 'Mais alors . . .' exclaimed Daniel Dechico the principal oboe, '. . . you 'ave played zis before?', on hearing the Welsh contingent making a passable rendering of Wagner's 'Siegfried Idyll' and Rossini's 'Italian Girl'. After that we were treated with genuine warmth and considerable respect by our French colleagues.

We were privileged to make music with some fine musicians, including Jean-Jacques Kantorow, then aged seventeen years, who played the Max Bruch Concerto beautifully, and, of course, our own Margaret Price.

Another incident which I shall not easily forget is arriving at Antibes in 1961 having been unable to find the whereabouts of the orchestra until the day of the first concert. I had practised the flute part of Bach's Brandenburg Concerto No.5 only to learn that the programme had been changed to the Brandenburg Concerto No.4 which I had never before played. Fortunately the Mayor of Cannes had invited us all to a meal before the concert which was extended by long speeches of welcome and accompanied by a most generous quantity of excellent *vin rouge*. I ignored the meal and the speeches (but not the excellent *vin rouge*) and hastily read through one of the two flute parts before launching into the Concerto on a bandstand in the middle of a square in Cannes – La-Bocca without any rehearsal but with a confidence extremely 'well-fortified'.

It is interesting to note that it was the foresight and effort of Irwyn Walters which made these concert tours such a success and so enjoyable, and which created an international musical experience which pre-dated the European Youth Orchestra by some fifteen years.

Michael O'Donoghue

Bains in the summer of 1959. Other courses followed in regular succession, with concerts given in French Riviera towns. There was even a Welsh concert at Swansea in the New Arts Hall of University College on 1 January 1963. One of the soloists there was Jean-Jacques Kantarow, winner of the Carl Flesch Gold Medal in 1962 and later of the Paganini Prize in Rome. He played Max Bruch's Concerto in G minor. Brenda Willoughby, a violin student at the RAM, and Daniel Dechico, an oboist in his third year at the Paris Conservatoire, played Bach's Double Concerto in C minor;

and the Welsh soprano Margaret Price, now celebrated worldwide, sang three songs composed by Irwyn's son Gareth Walters, whose earliest efforts at composition had been encouraged by Benjamin Britten when he had been a guest at the Walters's Swansea household in 1943. The final item in the 1963 concert comprised movements from Grace Williams's *Seven Scenes for Young Listeners*. In one remarkable sense the compositions by these last two close the circle, for Grace Williams had been for many years a fellow-student, intimate friend and musical confidante of Benjamin Britten. In 1961 Grace Williams wrote of Gareth Walters in *Welsh Music*, establishing his credentials as a former composition pupil of Olivier Messiaen in Paris. Recent successes, like the *Sinfonia Brève* and the *Divertimento* had enabled him to establish a style of his own, within which he had produced the songs sung by Margaret Price, *Poésies du soir* – settings of nineteenth-century French lyrics which eerily echo the youthful song-cycle that Britten had written nearly thirty years before, and which were not published or performed till after the English composer's death in 1976.

In 1965 the Franco-Welsh Orchestra was forced to change its name when it met for the first time in Italy. It then became known as the Societas Musica Europea, a title which more adequately expressed the new aim of enlisting musicians from countries other than France and Wales. Irwyn's foresight, then, was yet again in evidence, for it is interesting to note that this international venture started several years before the proposal to found a European Youth Orchestra was put to the European Community in 1974.

The Orchestra Franco-Galloise was by no means his only preoccupation during these post-NYOW years. Alun Davies, reporting on the Swansea National Eisteddfod, 1964, recorded his impressions of three concerts devoted to children and youth. In the first Irwyn conducted a performance of Fauré's *Requiem* by a massed choir of secondary-school children, though he thought 'the unnecessarily fast tempi did not reflect the distilled beauty of Fauré's serene and gentle conception of this Holy Office'. Fashions in music do change; and perhaps Irwyn's deep love of all things French and his realistic appreciation of the fragility of young voices had caused him to avoid over-stretching them by an insistence on prolonged sonority and extended vocal lines. (See Alun Davies, 'Report on the Swansea National Eisteddfod', *Welsh Music*, Vol. II, no. 7, Autumn 1964, 14.) At Swansea, too, there was an echo of Irwyn's pre-war past: Gwilym Roberts (surely with Irwyn's advice and support) conducted a staged performance of *Hiawatha* – this time with a thousand schoolchildren – which he had first conducted in Stafford as a young schoolmaster. The NYOW, under Raybould, also performed at the Swansea Eisteddfod, and Alun Davies thought that the highlight of their 'curiously selected programme' was Sibelius's *En Saga*.

Irwyn Walters retired from Her Majesty's Inspectorate in Wales in 1963. Within two years he was appointed Music Project Officer to the Disabled Living Foundation under the chairmanship of Lady Hamilton. When that assignment ended after a further two years he began working as examiner for the Trinity College of Music, starting in Canada and New Zealand, then continuing for several years with visits to South Africa, Australia, Hong Kong, Malaysia, Kenya, Singapore, Ceylon and India. During these tours, like his teacher David Vaughan Thomas, a Trinity College examiner nearly forty years before, he also gave lectures on music and the art of teaching.

VI The Second Phase: Transition and Change, 1958–1966

The 1958 course, then, was the first in which Irwyn Walters had not been actively involved in the administration of the NYOW. Perhaps Clarence Raybould had not clearly appreciated the heavy burden of work which Irwyn had been shouldering. His new dual duties were very demanding, particularly the annual task of auditioning prospective new members. He therefore decided to ask the WJEC that Welsh LEAs be invited to make a preliminary selection of students from their areas. By 1958, most counties had appointed music organizers or advisers, who had in many cases developed schemes for instrumental tuition and started their own county orchestras.

In some cases this had been a difficult task – for example, in Caernarvonshire, a county sixty miles from end to end. But, triumphing over the geographical problem, the music staff there organized weekend courses at Glynllifon in 1957 and 1958, under John Newman, who already had his own small orchestra at Pwllheli Grammar School where such activity had been fostered since the pioneering days of W. H. G. Jenkins in 1929. In 1959 a

The Monmouthshire Youth Orchestra with conductor Ronald Harding and Mrs Dorothy Adams-Jeremiah.

county youth orchestra was formed. Writing in 1961, Dorothy Adams-Jeremiah underlined the fact that, though the NYOW had been 'born in Monmouthshire' in 1946, that county had until then known little instrumental music, apart from its brass bands. 'The creation of the National Youth Orchestra in the county', she said, 'stimulated the urge to develop the orchestral side of music, and in the following year the first itinerant string teacher was appointed . . . Monmouthshire now has it own youth orchestra, with a second orchestra ready to move up as players leave.' (See Dorothy Adams-Jeremiah, 'Music in Education: 4. Monmouthshire', *Welsh Music* Vol. I no. 7, Winter 1961, 20.) Even Radnorshire, the most thinly populated Welsh county, with only six secondary schools, had managed to establish its own orchestra. In addition, it fed players into the Mid Wales Youth Orchestra, which in 1963 had as its director and tutor Irwyn's old Ammanford trio partner, Rae Jenkins, who had lately been conductor of the BBC Welsh Orchestra. At the other extreme of population size, the County Borough of Cardiff, from its youth orchestras, had supplied over 200 young players for the NYOW by 1963. One institution, in another county borough – Cyfarthfa Castle Grammar School, Merthyr Tydfil – had provided nearly ninety 'National' players over the same period. From those bare facts alone it is possible to determine with some accuracy the exfoliating influence, throughout Wales, of the original national ensemble which Irwyn Walters had created.

It was to the county music advisers who were sustaining these local ventures that Raybould was now constrained to turn. He convened a meeting in Cardiff, 15 January 1958, of musical representatives from each Welsh county. (These men and women, of course, would already have been very well known to Irwyn Walters, not simply through his management of the orchestra, but in his day-to-day role as HMI.) The music advisers were given the basic task of conducting the preliminary auditions to eliminate less able players. The finalists would be auditioned by Dr Raybould himself.

The help of the Guild for the Promotion of Welsh Music was also enlisted in the task of recommending suitable works by Welsh composers for inclusion in the NYOW programme, which would finally be determined by Dr Raybould. The list of such works already performed by the orchestra was most impressive. By the end of the Raybould era, it comprised:

1952   Fantasia on Welsh Nursery Tunes – Grace Williams
1953   Sea Sketches – Grace Williams

BBC recording at the City Hall, Cardiff, 1960.

1955   *Penillion* for Orchestra – Grace Williams*
1956   *Ieuenctid* – Daniel Jones*
1957   Fantasia for Orchestra – David Wynne*
1958   Fantasia for Orchestra – Arwel Hughes
1959   Four Welsh Dances – Alun Hoddinott
1960   Prelude for Orchestra – Arwel Hughes
1961   Tone Poem *The Dong with the Luminous Nose* – Robert Bruce
1962   Suite of Four Shakespeare Dances – Ian Parrott
        Two Welsh Nursery Tunes – Alun Hoddinott
1963   Variations for Orchestra – Alun Hoddinott*
1964   Overture *Hyfrydwch yr Ifanc* – Haydn Morris
        (* denotes a commission by the NYOW)

The first part of the 1958 summer course took place at the Llandrindod Wells Residential School, where there was a careful sifting to select a smaller orchestra for televised concerts, which represented a more musically satisfactory playing unit. The second course in Swansea was reserved for this more compact ensemble. The leader in 1958 was Anne Edwards from Anglesey; the soloists Elizabeth Vaughan, later to make an international reputation as an operatic soprano, and Ivor Bosanko (trumpet). Six concerts were given, including the customary performance at the National

Jeanette Massocchi, soloist with NYOW, 1961.

Eisteddfod. The orchestra appeared on BBC Television's *Concert Hour*, and a film of one of their earlier concerts was broadcast to schools in June, 1958.

Dr Raybould presented a verbal report to the WJEC at a meeting on 13 October 1958. He thanked his tutorial and administrative staff, and was particularly grateful for the help he had already received from county music advisers. He invited them to attend future courses, and in return welcomed invitations for him to hear performances by local and regional orchestras throughout the principality. But difficulties had arisen in north Wales because 'National' auditions had been arranged at short notice to fit into Dr Raybould's schedule: players had been auditioned for the first time and some had gained places without reference to their LEAs. It was agreed that in future the appropriate local authority should receive early information that a place was to be offered to a pupil, and would be asked by the secretary of the orchestra whether it agreed to take responsibility for the pupil's financial support. Problems also occurred when, during the course, students wished temporarily to lend their services to bands and local orchestras competing in the concurrent National Eisteddfod. In the past every effort had been made to grant these requests; but students' absence upset the homogeneous working of the NYOW and placed an additional strain upon the students. In some cases, the Eisteddfod required them to be absent from the course for several days. So the secretary agreed to ask the Eisteddfod committee to place preliminary and final competitions on the same day. Players selected for the 1959 course would be required to notify the secretary beforehand of their possible intention to enter National Eisteddfod competitions.

One of the conceptions of Ernest Read in London in the 1930s had been the creation of junior and senior youth orchestras. While conducting auditions for the 1958 course of the NYOW, Raybould became aware of the considerable number of promising young musicians for whom it was not possible to find a place in the orchestra. Older players could stay until they were twenty, which often left insufficient places for emerging talent. In these circumstances, it was thought, some of the younger candidates might be tempted to drift into the National Youth Orchestra of Great Britain, perhaps in the process turning the NYOW into a mere training ground for its imitative counterpart. It was suggested, therefore, that a second ensemble be created, to act as an 'incubator' for the main orchestra.

Rhoslyn Davies, Clarence Raybould's first assistant conductor.

The following proposals were put forward. The NYOW should be divided into two sections. Section A, numbering ninety to one hundred players, would comprise instrumentalists of the highest standard who might remain members to the upper age-limit if their playing standards were maintained. This section was to undertake the main concerts and broadcasts. Section B would comprise instrumentalists waiting for the opportunity of admission to section A. The main difficulty in implementing this scheme was that of accommodating extra players at the summer-course centres. Also, it would be necessary to appoint additional tutorial staff for the first part of each course. It was equally essential that a conductor be chosen to assist Dr Raybould with the second training orchestra.

This new vacancy was filled by Rhoslyn Davies, a supremely gifted young Welsh musician who, after graduating with a first-class honours degree at Aberystywth, had continued his studies at the Royal Academy, with conducting as his special subject. He had been appointed County Music Adviser for Montgomeryshire at the age of only twenty-four. In 1955 he won an Italian government scholarship and studied for a year in Rome before returning to London where he became assistant conductor to Colin Davis at Sadler's Wells. (In this connection it is interesting to note that Colin Davis had acted as wind tutor to the NYOW in 1955 and 1956.) After his first year with the NYOW, Rhoslyn Davies's promise was further confirmed: he was awarded a Federal Government Scholarship to study opera-conducting in West Germany. In the mean time, Raybould reported that the experiment with two orchestras was proving most successful. The 1959 course was attended by 174 students, of whom sixty-four belonged to the

It was the 1959 course held, I think, in the lovely spa town of Llandrindod Wells. Our opening item was *The Bartered Bride* overture by Smetana. A fiendishly fast and rhythmically treacherous piece, it collapsed at each rehearsal. (We never actually got through it although today's players would probably fly through this overture at first sight!)

On the eve of our first concert, at the Eisteddfod no less, and with morale sorely blighted by this wretched overture, we were amazed when Raybould instructed us all to go out and enjoy the night air! He 'looked forward to seeing us on the platform next evening'. Had the man gone mad we wondered? The usual mad dash to the pub did not occur that evening, strange as it may seem. Everyone, lofty principals included, spent the night feverishly practising that 'Blasted Bride', abject terror being a strong incentive.

So there we were, elegantly seated on the Eisteddfod platform like innocent lambs to the slaughter. Following a particularly sallow rendition of 'Mae Hen Wlad' we prepared to face the enemy. Consider our sense of chilled desolation when, after conducting the first few bars, Raybould calmly placed his hands behind his back and proceeded to smile benevolently at us while we frantically struggled to hold things together. Miracle of miracles, we actually did it! Only in the very last few bars did the Old Man pick up his discarded baton and, with a flourish, he brought the overture to a triumphal conclusion. The audience went wild with applause. If only they knew!

Raybould was later heard to say, 'I decided that if the little blighters won't play it with me, then they can damn well play it on their own.' And we did.

The influence of Clarence Raybould has remained with me until this very day. He was able to communicate his profound insight into the works studied in such a way as to inspire even the most diffident players in the back desks (where I began) to deliver of their best. His interpretation of the works of Sibelius (of whom he was a close friend) was spine-tingling. His eccentric trick in concerts of waving a white silk handkerchief to gain attention when things occasionally began to go astray was at once amusing and effective. Not unlike Beecham, our genial maestro was not averse to treating an inattentive audience to a cold stare. He was very tolerant of young people's inadequacies but despised pomposity and could offer an eloquent rebuke if necessary. He was a man blessed with 'the common touch' and I cherish a most vivid recollection of him sharing a cigar with an elderly pool attendant on the shore of the Menai Straits in Bangor while we, his wild children, cavorted in a rather decrepit swimming pool. They were great days!

Jeffrey Lloyd

B orchestra, learning the same repertoire but not takng part in concerts. Clarence Raybould felt that in Rhoslyn Davies he had found a man capable of implementing his own aspirations and requirements.

Raybould reported a continuing improvement in the orchestra's musical accomplishment, with which he was well pleased; especially since, with very few exceptions, the members were still at school or college, and, for the most part, were not considering a career in the musical profession. Nevertheless, he could assert that each year's course had revealed at least one person who subsequently had become a member of an established professional orchestra. In 1960, for instance, Geoffrey Gambould – a member of the NYOW from 1950 to 1954 – had been appointed principal bassoon in the BBC Symphony Orchestra.

By 1962 Rhoslyn Davies was thoroughly well established as Raybould's personal assistant in Wales and as a successful figure in Sadler's Wells. But it was during an engagement at the 1962 Coventry Festival that he died, at the tragically early age of thirty-five. Daniel Jones wrote of him:

> He died in the sound of a great Festival, and so the most promising of Welsh conductors passed away; . . . his passing has left Wales much the poorer . . . Here was a son of Wales and of the Rhondda Valley whose achievement was great, but whose promise was greater. It is a tragedy indeed that that promise can no longer be fulfilled. (*Welsh Music*, Vol. 2, no. 3.)

Rhoslyn Davies's untimely death meant that finding a replacement became a matter of great urgency. The WJEC approved Raybould's asking Arwel Hughes to assist him in the 1962 course, and his willingness to help was supported by the Welsh Department of the BBC, who agreed to release him temporarily from his duties as conductor of the BBC Welsh Orchestra. Another assistant, however, had to be found for 1963; and Raybould chose Arthur Davison, co-leader of the London Philharmonic Orchestra, whom he had first encountered as a Canadian student violinist at the Royal Academy in London. Under Davison's direction the B orchestra gave a short concert at the end of their week's work on the 1963 course, performing before the A orchestra as audience. This, by all accounts, was the best B orchestra to date. In the main concerts there was a newly commissioned work, Alun Hoddinott's *Variations for Orchestra*, dedicated to Dr Raybould, at whose invitation the composer conducted it in several concerts. *Variations* is divided into nine sections; the material heard in the first tutti is developed in the following variations, each of which gives prominence to one instrument or group of instruments, culminating in a final tutti. Raybould felt that the work made an attractive impression on audiences; and the orchestra had enjoyed playing it. Hoddinott was, incidentally, the first ex-member (also a founder-member) to have conducted the NYOW in a work of his own. Included in this year's programme, too, was an overture specially

Alun Francis (French horn), Jonathan Williams (clarinet), Wendy Sheppard (leader), Trevor Herbert (trombone), and Elizabeth Davies (cello), with Dr Raybould at Sophia Gardens, Cardiff, 1963.

composed for the orchestra by Haydn Morris, *Hyfrydwch yr Ifanc* (Joys of Youth), again dedicated to Clarence Raybould.

In 1963, also, there began a broadcasting saga of what turned out to be some considerable length. Derek Trimby of the BBC Features Department was permitted to make a film about the orchestra. With this in view, the final concert of the tour, at Cardiff, was recorded, together with some footage of their rehearsals at the Welsh College of Advanced Technology on 10 August. These events contributed to making the NYOW probably the most televised orchestra of its kind in the world.

On 3 November 1964 a conference of county music advisers was convened to exchange opinions about the orchestra's organization, with a particular view to forging closer links between the work of the advisers and the WJEC. It was suggested that each year one music adviser be invited to act as orchestral steward and librarian; and it was also proposed that the B orchestra be disbanded. In 1963 the reserve orchestra had numbered only thirty-seven, and it was considered that, since most counties now had their own effective youth orchestras, there were perfectly satisfactory opportunities for many players all over Wales to gain regular orchestral experience of a sufficiently high standard outside the NYOW summer courses.

The first phase of the 1965 course took place at Cartrefle College, Wrexham. Then the orchestra travelled to Cardiff Training College for their tour of south Wales. In December of this year Arthur Davison was officially named Dr Raybould's successor, chosen from a short list of seven candidates. He would take up his appointment on his predecessor's retirement in 1966, having recently resigned his post as co-leader of the London Philharmonic Orchestra to devote more time to conducting. Born in Canada, Arthur Davison began his mature studies at the Conservatoire de Musique in Montreal where he was awarded a scholarship to study at the Royal Academy in London; there he first met Clarence Raybould. He later became director of the Little Symphony of London, the Croydon Symphony Orchestra and the Royal Amateur Orchestral Society, and made frequent foreign conducting tours to Canada, New York and Copenhagen. In Britain he directed the RPO, the LPO, the Royal Liverpool Philharmonic Orchestra and the Bournemouth Symphony Orchestra, while giving special performances for young people at various centres in England.

In 1966 the NYOW was seeking to travel abroad once more, the recent failure to secure such visits having been largely due to financial difficulties. The NYOW's last foreign venture had been the highly successful tour of the Netherlands in 1957; since that had been Irwyn Walters's final direct contact with his orchestra, it might have seemed appropriate that this second continental visit should coincide with Clarence Raybould's last year in charge. The visit to West Germany in 1966 was organized by the WJEC with the assistance of the British Council, and arranged on an exchange basis. It also had considerable contemporary political significance, since in the previous year Queen Elizabeth had made an important ambassadorial tour of West Germany, on her return announcing that the British and West German governments were considering ways of encouraging youth exchanges between the two countries. The idea of a National Youth Orchestra of Wales had been conceived in 1944–5, the last year of hostilities, twenty-one years earlier. The members of the NYOW in 1966 had no memories of those war years, or even of their immediate aftermath, and therefore faced the tour with open minds, prepared to observe and judge for themselves. Their parents, however, who had experienced the hardships of the Second World War, may still have harboured rather different views of the venture. A spokesman for the orchestra, setting the tone for the tour, said, 'We are going to Germany to make music and friends.' The exchange was to be between the orchestra members and eighty-five German technical

Wendy Sheppard, Phyllis Hollington (trumpet), Wyn Edwards (trombone), John Williams (viola) and Michael Parrott (cello) with Dr Raybould.

students, who were simultaneously to visit industrial plants in south Wales.

A special course was held at Ogmore-by-Sea preparing for the continental visit during the three days before departure date. At the last minute it was announced that, on the advice of his doctor, eighty-year-old Clarence Raybould would not be travelling to Germany: Arthur Davison would conduct the orchestra.

It was arranged that the plane bringing the German students to Wales would return carrying the members of the NYOW. The tour began on a sour note when the aircraft arrived from Germany twelve hours behind schedule, and as a result the orchestra arrived in Stuttgart at midnight, somewhat fatigued after the trying delay, to begin an exhausting week of engagements. With an innocent confidence shared by many foreign touring ensembles in that era, the WJEC had trusted their overseas organizer, Ulrich Fauth, with arranging and assessing the venues, only to find that the halls were too small to accommodate the orchestra. The proposed concerts in Donaueschingen and Königsfeld consequently had to be cancelled.

The first concert was at Esslingen, on the evening after their arrival. It was a resounding success. The second was in the Gothic gabled city of Ulm on the Danube. Here, to the delight of the young visitors, a German children's choir sprang to their feet to sing *Mae Hen Wlad fy Nhadau* – in Welsh. It transpired that the Ulm choir had visited Wales on a number of occasions. Indeed, in

Germany there was already a 'tradition' of visits by musical groups to the post-war International Eisteddfod at Llangollen which had done much to heal lingering political wounds. For the first two concerts the orchestra had been accommodated in youth hostels; then they travelled to Schwenningen in the heart of the Black Forest where they stayed with local families who came *en masse* to hear their guests and award them an enthusiastic reception. It was generally agreed that Wales could have had no better ambassadors than those young musicians.

In 1966 the film which Derek Trimby had started to make two years earlier was shown on BBC Television. Entitled *Eighty Days to Make an Orchestra*, it included shots of planning and holding auditions, scenes at Wrexham railway station of the arrival of instrumentalists, and rehearsals before the Welsh tour began.

The 1966 summer course at Swansea College of Education was memorable on three accounts. It marked Clarence Raybould's twentieth year with the orchestra, his eightieth birthday, and, sadly for many, his retirement as conductor. This triple event merited a special report in *The Times* after the final concert at the National Eisteddfod in Port Talbot. This was a great occasion, epitomized, perhaps, by the orchestra's performance of another work commissioned from Alun Hoddinott. *The Times* judged that the 'Concerto Grosso No. 2 is a frank but enjoyable *pièce d'occasion* designed to show off each section of the orchestra. The players accepted the opportunities eagerly, bringing a youthful pride of possession and vitality to the performance.' At the end of the concert, B. G. Griffiths, the orchestra's administrator, paid tribute to Clarence Raybould, and the audience responded with a standing ovation.

Dr Clarence Raybould

Clarence Raybould's departure marked the end of the second era in the orchestra's history. The first episode – the orchestra's conception and establishment by Irwyn Walters – had undoubt-edly been of greater importance. But in the Raybould period, 1957–1966, the people of Wales almost reluctantly began to understand the significance of what had earlier been quietly and remarkably achieved. There arose an appreciation of the idea that the NYOW embodied the most substantial musical achievement in twentieth-century Wales, so far; and having been founded in the financially dessicated age of Stafford Cripps, it was frequently used as a rod to beat the back of Welsh complacency in the relatively affluent period of the 1960s. Its very originality and success threw into stark relief the continuing poverty of the remainder of Welsh musical achievement and aspiration.

In an editorial for *Welsh Music* in 1961 (I, 10, Autumn 1961), D. W. Davies argued that it was 'ludicrous' for a musical nation of two-and-a-half million people to have only one professional orchestra – the BBC Welsh Orchestra – of only forty-four players. 'Why cannot the BBC Welsh Orchestra be regarded as a nucleus for a full National Symphony Orchestra, and why cannot we recruit into it the cream of our instrumental talent from our ever increasing County and National Youth Orchestras? . . . Must we always survive on borrowed magic?' Later, in 1964, Davies wrote of 'the quiet revolution', the telling phrase which had been used in a BBC documentary to describe the 'phenomenal growth of instrumental music in the schools of Wales'. In a paroxysm of frustration, he went further and suggested that there was an illogicality in the achievement of Irwyn Walters, and his local orchestral disciples in Wales: 'The "Land of Song", against the odds, had produced the first National Youth Orchestra *in the world*; but the nation still had no national youth *choir*.' (*Welsh Music*, II, 7 Autumn 1964, 2.) We have had to wait twenty years for the fulfilment of that hope. But Davies's most substantial point, made in the early 1960s, was that Wales possessed seed-corn, in the form of the NYOW, but lacked the ground in which it might be further nurtured – a National Symphony Orchestra, a National Concert Hall, a National Opera House. None of these was being projected at that time, let alone implemented.

Aneurin Talfan Davies, in his report to the Guild for the Promotion of Welsh Music in 1960, uttered a more measured opinion:

> What stands in the way is the Welshman's traditional addiction to the dope of disunity – a disunity which inhibits growth and paralyses progress. This is to be regretted all the more because it happens at a time when the Welsh artist is proving his worth. In the world of music the last decade or so has shewn that Wales has a musical talent which is more than commensurate with its size. Welsh musicians are rapidly being recognised not only over the border, but on the concert platforms of Europe and the United States of America. (Report, Sixth Congress of the Guild for the Promotion of Welsh Music, Cardiff, 1960.)

It was perhaps the 'dope of disunity', in its political manifestation, which had ruthlessly eliminated Irwyn Walters from sharing in the fulfilment of his greatest conception, the NYOW, after 1957. Three years later, in 1960, D. W. Davies spoke of the orchestra as 'the brightest of Welsh candles' with 'not a single flicker in the flame' (*Welsh Music*, I, 7, Winter 1961, 2–3). The chief guardian of the tribal fire of youth, from 1966 until 1990, was to be Arthur Davison, known to later generations of the NYOW as 'The Godfather'.

VII   The Davison Era, 1966–1990

Clarence Raybould was an Englishman who had proudly relished his association with the National Youth Orchestra of Wales. In 1966 he must have felt deeply satisfied with its achievements during his twenty years as conductor. Many of the young players who had sat at his feet became well-known professional musicians and members of renowned orchestras. He therefore felt confident that, in handing over to Arthur Davison, he was ensuring the preservation of a grand tradition. The two men had worked together closely for four years; and Davison had a proven reputation for working skilfully with young musicians. The tutors from the previous year remained with the orchestra, thus guaranteeing continuity and the maintenance of high standards. Writing in *The Times*, 8 August 1968, of the NYOW at the Barry National Eisteddfod, Kenneth Loveland said,

Sir Arthur Davison

The concert, devoted largely to orchestral show-pieces, was exactly the kind of occasion which had established Mr Davison's reputation as a vigorous and successful trainer of young orchestral musicians, and was equally well designed to exhibit both the sectional and total virtuosity to which he has now brought this enthusiastic orchestra.

In 1969 the orchestra was invited to perform before the Prince of Wales in Cardiff during the investiture year. Before the concert in the New Theatre, a special training course took place, and a preliminary concert was given on 3 July at the Embassy Cinema, Bridgend. David Wynne wrote an arrangement of *Mae Hen Wlad fy Nhadau* to open the concert, and Alun Hoddinott was commissioned to compose an extended piece to commemorate the occasion, his second suite of *Welsh Dances*. (His first set of *Welsh Dances* Op. 22, had been commissioned earlier by the Royal Philharmonic Orchestra, also in commemoration of the investiture, receiving their first performance in London in June of that year.)

Lynne Thomas presenting Prince Charles with a stereo-recording of the NYOW after the investiture concert at the New Theatre, Cardiff, 1969.

A distinguished group of guests – including the Lord and Lady Mayoress of Cardiff, and the Secretary of State for Wales, George Thomas – sat with Prince Charles in the royal box. Mr Thomas reported that the prince had listened to the music with evident pleasure, nodding his head in time to the rhythm of the Mozart Symphony. A violin made in Llanfairfechan by a retired wood-work teacher, W. E. Pinnington, and ornamented with the arms of Caernarfon, was intended as a gift for the Prince of Wales; but it was passed on to Arthur Davison with the royal suggestion that the gift should be more suitably presented to a promising young violinist in the orchestra. A stereo-recording was made of the concert, and this was presented to the prince by Lynne Thomas from Felinfoel, a percussionist who had been in the orchestra since she was twelve years old, nine years before.

Two years later the orchestra celebrated its twenty-fifth anniversary. The WJEC commissioned Alun Hoddinott to write a work to commemorate the event; he said his Sinfonietta No. 4 was 'designed to show off the many talents and splendours of the National Youth Orchestra of Wales'. In 1970 the orchestra had recorded one side of a disc – to be released by HMV in the *Music for Pleasure* series – of Mussorgsky's *Pictures at an Exhibition*, in the Ravel orchestration. In 1971 they spent two further days recording Wagner's *Meistersinger* Overture and Hoddinott's Sinfonietta to complete the disc. Unfortunately the acoustics of the hall were unsatisfactory, and it was decided there would have to be a re-take in 1972.

The soloists for 1971 were Eluned Pierce (harp) and Gaynor

Gronow; but at the Eisteddfod concert on 4 August in Bangor, Osian Ellis, the celebrated harpist of the LSO, played Handel's Harp Concerto in B flat, while the other soloist was the tenor Wynford Evans. There were eight concerts in all. Osian Ellis went on record as saying that he would feel happier if more time were devoted to learning and less to concert-playing, since the members were, after all, students and not mature performers. A renowned soloist himself, his words recalled the controversy of 1958: 'I wish some means might be found to release the young instrumentalists for two or three days, and indeed that they might be encouraged to contribute to the Eisteddfod by taking part in its competitions. At present, due to their commitment to the Youth Orchestra, Welsh instrumentalists are not able to compete in the Eisteddfod' (*Western Mail* report). The point was fairly made; for the quality of instrumental competitions at the Eisteddfod was sure to be affected by the absence of such a large cohort of talented players on orchestral courses.

Urdd Gobaith Cymru (the Welsh League of Youth) was due to celebrate its fiftieth anniversary in 1972, and the wish was communicated to the WJEC that William Mathias be commissioned to compose an appropriate work for performance by the NYOW at their concerts that year. Their offer was gratefully accepted. Mathias's suite of *Celtic Dances* Op. 60 consisted of four sections concerned with mythical rituals and celebrations. The composer said he had intended to capture something of the vitality and optimism of youth, while producing a work which would please players and audiences alike. Later the orchestra spent two days recording the *Celtic Dances*, along with Shostakovich's 'Festival Overture', in order to complete the disc originally begun in 1970. Released in 1973, it was greeted by a clutch of very favourable reviews. The *Gramophone*, the leading British journal of its kind for the previous fifty years, commented on the record, in July 1973:

> If it is a demonstration of how astonishingly well a good youth orchestra can play a very difficult score, then the performance is a tribute to the skill of these young players . . . it is an outstanding youth orchestra . . . They are well tuned (not always to be said of young players, some of whom are likely to have poor instruments anyway) and they are well blended. Brass and percussion are generally first-rate . . . [This is] certainly a great achievement for Arthur Davison and his young players.

If anything, the review in *Records and Recording* (August 1973) was even more fulsome.

The Mussorgsky is a powerful interpretation; Arthur Davison who obviously has a genius for conducting youth orchestras, judges his tempi so that they are within the players' capabilities yet stretch them to the full, and of course young performers relish being stretched to the limits of their capabilities, as long as they are not exceeded. They have some superb soloists (the tuba in *Bydlo*, and the trumpet in *Samuel Goldenberg and Schmuyle* spring to mind as knocking spots off some of their professional competitors on record, and they are not the only ones), the recording itself is admirably polished and focused, and the whole thing is highly competitive.

As a result of this success, the WJEC received an invitation from EMI for the orchestra to record film music by twentieth-century composers.

On 27 March 1972 Clarence Raybould died at Bideford General Hospital, where he had been receiving treatment for a diabetic condition. He was eighty-five years old, and six years had passed since his retirement as conductor of the NYOW. Few, if any, then, of the 1972 membership would have remembered him personally; but Arthur Davison, his friend and associate, mourned the passing of one who had devoted so much time and energy to bringing the orchestra to a pitch of excellence.

In the same year plans were initiated for another foreign tour to take place in 1973, immediately after the customary circuit of concerts in Wales. Visits to the Netherlands in 1957 and West Germany in 1966 had been highly successful; but the 1973 tour was to be different: based on a cruise ship, the orchestra would stop off to give concerts in four different countries. The 1973 course began at Cartrefle on 26 July. After completing their north Wales tour, the players travelled to Swansea College of Education. On 26 August the orchestra boarded the educational cruise ship *Uganda* at Tilbury. The Welsh party included WJEC officials and a BBC television crew. Preliminary arrangements for the concerts *en route* had been made by P.&O., but in the light of difficulties experienced in 1966, Arthur Davison had personally inspected the concert halls beforehand to satisfy himself as to their suitability. Concerts were to be given in Oslo, Hamburg, Antwerp and De Montivilliers, near Le Havre. Some of the concerts were recorded by Scandinavian and Belgian television crews for later transmission.

The sea voyage in itself was a cause of great excitement among the players. Dr Huw Griffiths, an oboist in the NYOW from 1970 to 1973, recalls that, since there were many young children among the ordinary passengers on the educational cruise, the P.&O.'s appointed 'headmaster', a lean, pale man with a small dark

1973 members' cruise.

moustache, insisted on the first evening that everyone be in bed by 9 p.m., seriously overlooking the comparative maturity of many members of the orchestra. The passage to Norway was so stormy that even some of the crew-members admitted to feeling ill. Bravely, however, Arthur Davison called a rehearsal of the Sibelius Symphony in one of the ship's lounges, as Huw remembers (in a letter to the author): 'There was a rather poor turn-out, even at the start, and as time went on, fewer and fewer people remained in their seats as more and more succumbed to sea-sickness. The scene was more reminiscent of Haydn's "Farewell" Symphony than Sibelius.' The ambassadorial members of the orchestra even managed to deal diplomatically with the 'headmaster':

After the first evening aboard the ship the 9 p.m. curfew had been relaxed, and on most evenings we were allowed to hold a 'senior club' with a disco and soft drinks. There was even a happy reconciliation with the Headmaster who, on being tackled (verbally) by a few plucky members of the woodwind section, responded by inviting them to his cabin for a glass of whisky.

The press response to the orchestra, wherever it went on this tour, was beyond all measure enthusiastic. Under the headline, 'Youth Orchestra of Wales Amazes Antwerp', the Belgium daily *De Standard* remarked,

. . . For the Orchestra and also for what it accomplished only one word is appropriate: 'Fantastic' . . . An Orchestra which is barely one month old, and which will soon disappear into nothingness again, demonstrated an orchestral discipline and maturity which is not always shown by professional orchestras with established reputations . . . What this Orchestra achieved in fine phrasing in Sibelius's Second Symphony was as moving as it was surprising.

De Standard described in some detail the orchestra's history, how the players were selected and their mode of rehearsing. But it was the playing which left the deepest impression: 'The sounds of different sections blend together, the nuances are carried through to the utmost degree, and every performance is a wonder of orchestral finesse.' This was an orchestra 'never to be forgotten'.

In the Oslo *Aftenpost* on 28 August 1973, Dag Winding Sørenson, a Norwegian musician of international standing, summed up the whole achievement of the NYOW since 1946:

> It is well known that the Welsh are a singing nation, but the National Youth Orchestra of Wales which played in the University Hall yesterday gave evidence that there is reason to believe that the standard of instrumental music is in no way inferior in Wales. The Orchestra consists of 140 young musicians between 13 and 21 years of age – almost twice as many as the Oslo Philharmonic Orchestra . . . The programme states that only a small number of players intend becoming professional musicians, but in spite of this the Orchestra attains an extraordinary high standard. The first part of the concert consisted of characteristic orchestral bravura pieces, from Wolf-Ferrari's Overture *Susannah's Secret* to the lively *Investiture Dances* of Alun Hoddinott and the Rimsky-Korsakov *Capriccio Espagnol* . . . The Conductor, Arthur Davison, who did not spare his musicians, showed how far he dared drive them in the gigantic task offered by Sibelius's Symphony No. 2 in D major.

Arthur Davison's growing reputation was reinforced by the granting of several awards over the next few years; in 1973, an EMI/CFP award marking the sale of half-a-million of his own classical recordings; in 1974 the honorary degree of Master of Music of the University of Wales, and a CBE for his services to music; and in 1976 the Guild for the Promotion of Welsh Music's John Edwards Memorial Award for long and distinguished service to music in Wales.

B. G. Griffiths, who had been the orchestra's administrator for many years, died suddenly in 1977. He had befriended and inspired hundreds of orchestra members. Gareth Wood was commissioned to compose a fanfare as a tribute to him and in

Alun Hoddinott

memory of his immeasurable services to the NYOW, and this was played at the beginning of each concert that season.

In the late 1970s there was a shift in national educational policy which switched the emphasis in the schools service away from broad curricular aims to a narrower concern with vocational and economic needs. This was a time, for instance, of rising juvenile unemployment and runaway inflation in the public and private sectors; and spending in the education service was being examined far more critically than ever before in post-war Britain: the fashionable word in education became 'accountability' – the measurement of the product of educational investment. The splendid effects of the achievement of the NYOW over three decades was surely plain for all to see; but those effects could not be accurately measured by accountants. In 1979 the WJEC was told by the government that further cuts in spending had to be made in the education service over the next two years. A consequence of these proposed economies would be that the NYOW, together with the recently created National Youth Theatre of Wales and the splendid National Museum Schools Service, would no longer receive sufficient public funds to guarantee their continuance. The Welsh LEAs sent a deputation to the Welsh Office, where Mr Michael Roberts was under-secretary responsible for education, to plead for a change of heart. Raymond Edwards, Principal of the Welsh College of Music and Drama, wrote at this time, 'We cannot allow the Youth Orchestra and Theatre to go. If the local authorities insist that they cannot afford them, then other ways and means of financing them must be found.' Professor Alun Hoddinott, a founder-member of the NYOW, a composer of international renown, and now Head of the Music Department at University College, Cardiff, said: 'This Orchestra has had a great influence on the musical scene in Wales and has been an important ambassador abroad for the country. It represents the pinnacle of all achievements in youth music and gives young people something to aim for which helps them to develop their ability. It just can't be allowed to perish' (*Western Mail* report).

At this critical juncture, and in response to appeals for financial aid, the Secretary of State for Wales, Nicholas Edwards, made a grant of £10,000, and the Welsh Arts Council contributed a further £3,750 to ensure that the 1980 course and concerts could take place. But it was necessary to make additional plans for subsequent years. The Arts Council arranged for a seminar on sponsorship to be conducted in Cardiff, and this was attended by over 100 people. John Brace, Secretary of the WJEC, attended and gained valuable information about sponsorship. The orchestra was in a relatively

Carys Hughes, Gwawr Owen, Gwenllian Rowlands, and Rhian Williams (left to right), 1981.

strong position since it could offer considerable advertising benefits to potential sponsors through this annual schedule of travelling concerts. In the immediate event the orchestra was saved by a generous grant of £36,000 from BP Chemicals for the next three years. A BP spokesman explained that such sponsorship was in line with their policy of encouraging and supporting youthful endeavour in many fields. So in 1981 the logo of the orchestra, which had appeared on concert programmes since 1949, was replaced by the Red Dragon, the insignia of the main sponsors of the NYOW, British Petroleum.

As if to acknowledge the recent rescue and renewed vitality of the orchestra, in 1982, with funds donated by the Welsh Arts Council, another work was commissioned from Alun Hoddinott. He dedicated his *Five Studies for Orchestra* to the NYOW. As with his earlier *Variations*, each of the five episodes explored a particular aspect of orchestral playing, and the principals of every section were featured in cadenza passages.

In 1982 BP conveyed the valuable news to the WJEC that their sponsorship would continue for the next six years. That year, too, was marked by the celebration of Arthur Davison's twenty-one years of association with the orchestra. Wayne Warlow, who had been principal cellist with the NYOW in earlier years, directed a one-hour film for Dinas Productions which was to be shown on S4C, the new Welsh-medium television channel. It portrayed the

NYOW 1980: saved by BP sponsorship.

whole process of preparation for the 1983 course and the subsequent concerts. Warlow also invited ex-members of the orchestra to meet to discuss the possibility of forming an association, the purpose of which would be twofold: continuing social contact among former players, and the provision of extra support for the orchestra. This and the extension of BP's sponsorship not only gave it a vital lifeline, but represented the affection in which the NYOW was held by hundreds of ex-members.

In 1987 Alun Hoddinott was asked to write a work in celebration of Arthur Davison's twenty-five years with the NYOW. The critic of the *South Wales Echo* reported that the performance of *Improvisation on an Old Welsh Tune* had made a 'stunning impact', with moments of 'deep mystery . . . When the tune finally comes through, it is like a ray of sunshine.'

Financial restrictions had precluded foreign touring since 1973. But in 1988, with help from a variety of sponsors, in addition to BP, a second visit to West Germany was arranged. During their stay at Cologne, Tony Moore, now Head of Music at Bryncelynnog Comprehensive School, vividly remembers 'The Godfather' being whisked around the city in a black Mercedes. The first German concert was on 5 August in the beautiful setting of the open-air market place in Bonn. On a lovely evening the audience included customers in the bars and restaurants surrounding the square,

In the first violins sectional room we anxiously awaited the arrival of our tutor, Miss Vera Kantrovitch. She arrived: short, plump, with bright black beady eyes – eyes which showed us clearly enough that discipline was of the utmost importance! Having each performed individually and been placed within the section, we settled down to study the scores . . . She didn't waste time repeating passages which were well within our scope, but rather led us along the route of mastering apparently unplayable phrases and sharing with us some 'tricks of the trade' . . . 'Aunty Vera', as we fondly called her, allocated to each of us the name of an animal which we apparently resembled. I seemed to change animals regularly, but there were a few others who remained the same. I often wonder whether the section still contains such a mélange of species as during my days with the orchestra.

I had never before come across anyone with such charisma. He [Arthur Davison] had only to enter the room to have all our attention. Admittedly terror played a great part in our awe, but this was quickly transformed into respect. We were swept along on a tide of adrenalin, and woe betide anyone caught playing after the final downbeat. 'In this Orchestra there's only the quick and the dead!' – and we made sure there were only the quick! [He] was a wonderful musician and we were lucky to have had the opportunity of working with him in the NYOW ('Streets ahead of the NYOGB', as he never ceased assuring us!)

Elenid Owen

though the performance was in no way marred by the congenial chink of beer glasses and plates in the neighbouring pavement cafés. Elenid Owen, soloist and leader of the orchestra, spoke fluent German and acted as compère for the tour. At that time she was studying with Igor Ozim at the Musikhochschule in Cologne. The Bonn concert ended with Johann Strauss's 'Thunder and Lightning' Polka which was several times encored, the audience clapping in time to the music. Concerts were given on the following two days at the luxurious Sports and Leisure Complex at Bad Nauheim and at Bad Neuenahr, another health resort, where the concert hall was the best during this tour. Both audiences responded warmly to the high quality of the performances. On 9 August the last concert took place at Gemund, fifty miles south-west of Cologne, where the orchestra received a standing ovation. Dirk Sieper, the local cultural director, declared the concert to be 'the cultural event of the Jubilee Year in Gemund'.

There was a special concert at St David's Hall, Cardiff, later in the year on 23 November. This was sponsored by Vimto as part of a two-day programme of events associated with the Duke of

Arthur Davison with leader
Carl Darby, 1980.

Edinburgh's Award Scheme. Huw Rhys Evans (tenor) and Elenid Owen were the soloists.

The year 1990 was Arthur Davison's last – his twenty-eighth year – as conductor of the orchestra. The 1990 course was based in the city of Gloucester, and from there the players travelled to give concerts in Carmarthen, the Rhymney National Eisteddfod, Birmingham and Cardiff. A new work, Sinfonietta No. 4, by Gareth Wood, a former member then playing double bass in the RPO, was commissioned to mark Arthur Davison's retirement, and was dedicated to him in gratitude for all the years of devoted service he had rendered to the NYOW. The atmosphere at the last concert of the tour, in St David's Hall, Cardiff, was charged with emotion. Michael Bell's report in the *Western Mail*, on 11 August, gives some indication of this, especially in his remarks on the performance of Sibelius's Second Symphony:

> Throughout the symphony, the expressive power of the strings was a joy to hear . . . The young musicians played their hearts out until the final emotionally-charged climax was reached, and this was quite overwhelming in its power and grandeur – a fitting climax to Arthur Davison's last appearance with the National Orchestra of Wales.

Aldon Rees, in his reflections on Gareth Wood's Sinfonietta at the earlier Carmarthen concert, touched on another cause for regret:

> This year's commissioned work . . . is tinged with sadness, not only for its Swan Song dedication to Davison, but also its elegiac middle movement in recent memory of Haydn Wyn Davies, a founder-member of the Orchestra, a truly unforgettable and characterful musician with a life of music-making in Wales.

Haydn Wyn Davies's life of selfless dedication to Welsh music in the post-war years reflects the broad and profound effect which the NYOW and many of its members have had upon the general musical life of Wales. And in his professional career there were interesting parallels with that of his predecessor, Irwyn Walters. Haydn Davies, a founder-member, had been principal cellist and horn-player in the orchestra (followed a few years later by his sister, Helena). He taught for fifteen years in Pontypridd where he diffused his immense musical vitality among choirs and orchestras in the region. Moving to north Wales, as music adviser for Caernarvonshire (later Gwynedd), he revitalized that county in similar ways, orchestral and choral. Finally, while an HMI for music, working out of Aberystwyth, he continued his active involvement in music-making of various kinds.

The subsequent careers of other former members of the NYOW have followed a similar pattern, particularly in the field of youth-orchestra activity. Haydn Davies's sister, Helena Braithwaite, as music adviser, has made the county of South Glamorgan a centre of musical excellence unequalled throughout Britain, with a battery of school and youth orchestras, brass and wind groups and choirs which achieve ever-better standards of performance. Jeffrey Lloyd, sometime leader of the NYOW, has carried into the schools of South Glamorgan the enthusiasm initially engendered when he attended his first National Youth Orchestra course in the 1950s. Those are simply good examples taken at random from a potentially long list. In every Welsh county there are keen peripatetic instrumental teachers – former members of the National Youth Orchestra in many cases – who spread the word of the ultimate pleasure and satisfaction of participation in orchestral performance of considerable quality. The NYOW, in other words, has not simply functioned since 1946 as a constantly changing band of the very best young instrumentalists: it has had the much more worthwhile effect of transforming – by means of a 'quiet revolution' – the lives of countless numbers of ordinary schoolchildren, in the process giving instrumental music a place in Welsh culture which is surely one of the most important developments to have taken place during this century in Wales. And at the very highest level of musical accomplishment, the NYOW has provided a platform for displaying the creative gifts of at least three generations of Welsh composers: Daniel Jones and Grace Williams; Alun Hoddinott and William Mathias; Gareth Walters and Gareth Wood.

Over thirty years ago, commenting on what the NYOW had even then begun to achieve, D. W. Davies wrote:

The importance of the individual has always been a traditional characteristic of Welsh life and culture. This is particularly true, for example, of the development of education in Wales and of her major educational establishments: they were built *by* the people; they remain *of* the people. The same is true of her cultural achievements, particularly in music . . .' (Editorial, *Welsh Music*, I, 8, 1961, 3–4.)

Viscount Tonypandy unveiling the memorial plaque to Irwyn Ranald Walters at a special concert held in his memory at Haberdashers' Monmouth School for Girls. On the left is Irwyn's son Gareth Walters.

It can truly be said that historic and continuing achievement of the National Youth Orchestra of Wales is still traceable to one individual – to his vision in conceiving of it, to his desire to restore a sense of balance in the musical life of the nation, and to his administrative persistence in pushing his ideal to fulfilment. Irwyn Walters's infuence upon the musical lives of the young people of Wales will continue for as long as his orchestra survives; and, of course, it will also be embodied in the living tradition which he established among the hundreds of music teachers whose interest and enthusiasm were first awakened by his visionary achievement. It is hoped that this book, dedicated to his memory, will help to restore him to a properly pre-eminent place in the history of Welsh music. An appropriate epitaph for his work is embodied in a remark written by Huw Williams in 1968:

> It should be remembered that our National Youth Orchestra, our major orchestral works, our ambitious music festivals, and even live performances of the masterpieces of our own composers, were until quite recently very idle dreams'. (*Welsh Music*, III, 2, Spring 1968, 14.)

Coda: Past and Future

On the retirement of Arthur Davison, Elgar Howarth was appointed conductor of the orchestra for an agreed period of five years. When Howarth was unable to attend the beginning of his first summer course, due to prior commitments, a former member of the orchestra, Michael Thomas (more familiarly know to his contemporaries as 'Tom Pitch', for his gift of perfect pitch) acted as training conductor, having previously been acknowledged as Arthur Davison's right-hand man. Inspector for Schools in the Borough of Croydon, he was geographically close enough to Davison's home to make their mutual musical involvement practicable. His association with the NYOW had lasted twenty-nine years. From 1963 to 1969 he played the viola, subsequently acting as librarian and orchestra steward. Michael Thomas's long years of service represent the camaraderie which has been sustained among so many members.

Elgar Howarth

Arthur Davison died, in August 1992, at the age of seventy-four. His memorial concert at Fairfield Halls, Croydon, on 27 November, was attended by many young people with whom he had worked during his twenty-eight years with the orchestra. The music critic of the *South Wales Echo*, A. J. Sicluna, described Davison as a gentle giant who could make young orchestral players sound like angels. Some other critics have suggested that the repertoire chosen for the orchestra in his time was somewhat limited, and that certain favoured works appeared at frequent intervals. But at his final concert, for instance, Shostakovich's 'Festival' Overture provided an exciting opening, and was followed by Gareth Wood's newly commissioned Sinfonietta 4.

Davison's successor, Elgar Howarth, is widely known as an exponent of twentieth-century music. On his appointment, the orchestra moved into a new era. As a pupil at Eccles Grammar School, near Manchester, he was taught by the pianist Ron Dawson and the clarinetist Geoffrey Varley, whom Howarth recalls as a dynamic and determined musician. Like many northern players Howarth was nurtured in the true brass-band tradition by his father, conductor of the Barton Hall Band. In the 1950s he went on to study music at Manchester University, where Peter Maxwell

Davies, Alexander Goehr and John Ogdon were among his contemporaries. His conducting career began to flourish in the 1970s, and he has worked with all the leading orchestras in the country. His international career has included directing the world première of Ligeti's *Le Grand Macabre* in Stockholm. Opera remains his consuming passion, together with a wide swathe of twentieth-century music, and he continues to compose, especially for brass. In 1988 he published a lively history of the brass-band tradition, *What a Performance!* His abiding interests are reflected in the repertoire he has chosen for the NYOW, particularly the Michael Blake Trumpet Concerto which was written for Håkan Hardenberger who had given its première in 1989 with the Bournemouth Symphony Orchestra. Further challenges have been presented to orchestra and audiences alike with, for instance, Lutoslawski's *Mi-Pariti* in 1993 and Ligeti's *Macabre Collage* in 1994.

The year 1995 heralds the fiftieth anniversary of the inception of the National Youth Orchestra of Wales. Celebrations will include masterclasses, workshops and a tour lasting through the month of August. The great instrument created by Irwyn Ranald Walters continues to resonate passionately throughout the musical life of Wales at the end of the twentieth century.

Appendix I: Founder Members of the National Youth Orchestra of Wales, 1946

Alun Baxendale
Betty Bowen
Auriol Bryant
Terence Burke
Blodwen Butcher
Walter Cahill
Margaret Chiverton
Doland Clarke
Jean Collings
Janet Craxton
Gareth Davies
Gwyn Davies
Haydn Davies
John Davis
Dylis Dodd
Osian Ellis
Betty Evans
Noel Evans
Gareth Griffiths
John Harris
Oswald Henry
Alun Hoddinott
Mavis Hopkins
Francis Howard
John Howard
Derek James

Leonard James
Dilwyn Jenkins
Gordon Jenkins
Geraint John
Arvona Jones
David Arwyn Jones
Glanmor Jones
Graham Jones
Hugh Jones
Ifor Jones
Menai Jones
Rene Jones
Shirley Jones
Joan Lewis
Elinor Leyshon
Joan Llewellyn
Norman Mason
Arthur Morgan
Joan Morris
Harold Nash
John Newman
Terence Patten
George Pheocritoff
Bryan Pollard
Evan Price
Merlin Pritchard

Brenda Rees
John Rees
Richard Rees
Gerald Reynolds
R. E. Reynolds
David Richards
Gerald Richards
Emlyn Roberts
Janet Simm
Hilary Squire
Patrick Stephens
Nancy Sweet
Glenna Thomas
Mary Thomas
Thesca Thomas
Brenda Tuck
Gareth Walters
Sylvia Watkins
Alun Way
Gerald Webb
Gerald Wiesbard
C. K. Williams
Elizabeth Williams
John Wood

Appendix II: National Youth Orchestra of Wales: List of Members, 1951–1990

Note: The earliest available records of orchestra members are the lists of names printed in concert programmes from 1951 onwards. The following list of members has been compiled from information printed in concert programmes from 1951 to 1990 (i.e., up until the end of the 'Davison era'). Orchestra members who have played more than one instrument are listed for each instrument played. Members who have changed address may be listed more than once.

Forename	Surname	Instrument	Year	Town
Penelope	Abbott	Oboe	1961	Margam
Martin	Abraham	Violin	1979	Bridgend
Craig	Adams	Horn	1989	Abertillery
Gareth	Adams	Violin	1961	Pontypridd
Glynne	Adams	Violin	1984	Llanymynech
Kevin	Adams	Violin	1969	Pontypridd
Valerie	Adams	Violin	1952	Abertillery
Christine	Afan-Jones	Violin	1964	Port Talbot
Geraldine	Affley	Double bass	1956	Cardiff
Philip	Aird	Violin	1985	Pontypridd
Perys Wyn	Alban	Harp	1982	Colwyn Bay
Ronald	Alban	Violin	1952	Merthyr Tydfil
Peter	Alcock	Bassoon	1980	Llanfairfechan
Philip	Alexander	Clarinet	1981	Ystradgynlais
Joy	Alford	Viola	1953	Milford Haven
Graham	Allport	Violin	1959	Barry
Jane	Alwyn	Viola	1963	Newport
Gwilym	Ambrose	Cello	1959	Caerleon
Julie	Ambrose	Violin	1970	Llandeilo
Anthony	Anderson	Violin	1980	Penmaenmawr
John	Anderson	Oboe	1969	Pennard
Carl	Andrews	Violin	1960	Neath
Roger	Andrews	Double bass	1957	Cardiff
Bethan	Annwel	Harp	1983	Llanbrynmair
Elizabeth	Anthony	Percussion	1967	Llanelli
Susan	Anthony	Double bass	1961	Pontypool
Roger	Argente	Trombone	1979	Neath
Jeffrey	Armes	Cello	1954	Milford Haven
Margaret	Artus	Violin	1951	Bodfari
Michael	Ashley	Violin	1988	Cardiff
Christopher	Ashmead	Viola	1974	Bryncoch
Gareth	Ashmead	Violin	1980	Neath
Ann	Ashton	Cello	1981	Pendyrys
Sian	Ashton	Violin	1988	Nantyglo
Simon	Ashton	Violin	1985	Cardiff
Simon	Aspell	Viola	1979	Swansea
Roger	Astley	Flute	1970	Metford
Janice	Atherton	Percussion	1983	Colwyn Bay
Anthony	Atkins	Percussion	1958	Cardiff
Robert	Atkins	Horn	1978	Abertillery
John	Atkinson	Trombone	1953	Deganwy
Patricia	Atkinson	Oboe	1958	Cardiff
Graham	Attwood	Bassoon	1951	Gowerton
D. Roland	Aubrey	Double bass	1954	Llanelli

Benjamin	Averis	Bassoon	1972	Welshpool
Michael	Axtell	Flute	1959	Skewen
David	Ayres	Cornet	1957	Trebanos
Gordon	Back	Viola	1966	Neath
Marilyn	Bacon	Flute	1963	Holyhead
Vernon B.	Bailey-Wood	Violin	1952	Porth
Nicholas	Baldwin	Violin	1981	Pontypridd
Rebecca	Ball	Cello	1988	Cardiff
Sian	Ball	Oboe	1986	Cardiff
Ian	Balmain	Trumpet	1978	Wrexham
Sheena	Balmain	Clarinet	1977	Wrexham
Andrew	Barker	Trombone	1985	Caergwrle
Sian	Barnes	Cello	1984	Caernarfon
Nicholas	Barr	Viola	1982	Cardiff
Sara	Barratt	Oboe	1988	Aberystwyth
Eleanor	Barry	Violin	1989	Bassaleg
Eileen	Bartlett	Double bass	1957	Kingsbridge
Penny	Barton	Clarinet	1975	Barry
Sarah	Barton	Cello	1976	Barry
Denise	Bassett	Violin	1951	Rhoose
Ian	Bassett	Double bass	1956	Llanelli
Mary	Bate	Viola	1957	Cardiff
Martin	Bates	Double bass	1977	Bow Street
Andrew	Bather	Trombone	1977	Conwy
Angela	Beard	Double bass	1973	Welshpool
Nicholas	Beard	Cello	1986	Newport
Roy	Beavon	Trumpet	1953	Machynlleth
Andrew	Beazley	Violin	1983	Swansea
Mansel	Bebb	Violin	1957	Tir-phil
John	Beckett	Viola	1964	Llanelli
Nigel	Beddoe	Violin	1980	Tonyrefail
Graham	Beer	Bassoon	1962	Montgomery
Stephen	Begley	Viola	1983	Caerphilly
Catherine	Bell	Cello	1970	Colwyn Bay
Avril	Bendall	Double bass	1963	Porthcawl
Stephen	Benevente	Clarinet	1966	Newport
Hywel	Benjamin	Violin	1971	Neath
Elizabeth	Bennett	Flute	1968	Fishguard
Malcolm	Bennett	Clarinet	1989	Brecon
Richard John	Bennett	Violin	1989	Merthyr Tydfil
Anna Lea	Benson	Violin	1987	Marford
Nigel	Beresford	Violin	1963	Bridgend
Lionel	Berrigan	Cello	1953	Haverfordwest
Sarah	Betty	Horn	1985	Cwmbrân
Anthony	Bevan	Viola	1956	Llanelli
Christopher	Bevan	Violin	1968	Newtown
Janet	Bevan	Violin	1969	Llanelli
Nia	Bevan	Violin	1988	Cardiff
Richard John	Bevan	Horn	1989	Hawarden
Sian	Bevan	Viola	1987	Cardiff
Darren Sinclair	Beynon	Trumpet	1986	Wrexham
Irene	Beynon	Violin	1964	Newport
Justin	Beynon	Bassoon	1960	Cardiff
Kathleen	Bibby	Violin	1957	Colwyn Bay
Frances	Binding	Viola	1978	Carmarthen
Ruth	Bingham	Cello	1985	Mold
Vivien	Birdsall	Violin	1981	Swansea
Helen	Bishop	Clarinet	1977	Caldicot
Susan	Bishop	Clarinet	1975	Caldicot
John A.	Blackmore	Oboe	1951	Cardiff
Janet	Blackwell	Violin	1958	Newport
Richard	Blewett	Clarinet	1970	Newport
Simon	Blore	Trumpet	1982	Wrexham
Nigel	Blundell	Double bass	1961	Welshpool

Morwen	Blythin	Harp	1984	Rhuddlan
George	Boardman	Cello	1952	Cricieth
Mansel	Bobb	Violin	1956	Tir-phil
Margaret	Bolton	Viola	1959	Cwmbran
John	Bond	Viola	1956	Port Talbot
Leon	Bond	Trumpet	1984	Llandrindod Wells
Ivor	Bosanko	Trumpet	1954	Cardiff
Rachel	Bott	Violin	1987	Aberystwyth
Alan	Bourne	Trumpet	1983	Pembroke
Raymond	Bowden	Flute	1959	Neath
Beryl	Bowen	Oboe	1951	Griffithstown
Catherine Rhian	Bowen	Violin	1988	Aberdare
D. Lawrence	Bowen	Cello	1957	Trebanos
Glyn	Bowen	Trombone	1978	Ammanford
Gregory	Bowen	Trumpet	1957	Llangennech
Gwenallt	Bowen	Flute	1990	Llangennech
J. Elwyn	Bowen	Violin	1956	Swansea
Jean	Bowen	Violin	1964	Berriew
John Edgar	Bowen	Violin	1952	Swansea
Martin	Bowen	Bassoon	1970	Neath
Mervyn	Bowen	Violin	1960	Berriew
Thomas	Bowen	Trombone	1982	Ammanford
Windor	Bowen	Trombone	1957	Pennard
Jane	Bower	Violin	1956	Ebbw Vale
Anne	Bowles	Cello	1956	Pontypool
Philip	Boyden	Violin	1985	Rogerstone
Gillian	Brace	Violin	1967	Southerndown
Susan	Brace	Violin	1961	Llanelli
Gillian Lee	Bradley	Violin	1986	Abergavenny
Hillary	Braime	Double bass	1975	Newport
John Ellis	Braithwaite	Tuba	1980	Welshpool
Vivienne	Braithwaite	Flute	1985	Cardiff
Gillian	Brance	Violin	1966	Southerndown
Paula	Brice	Oboe	1968	Cwmbran
Paul	Bridger	Violin	1954	Swansea
Robert	Bridges	Horn	1952	Rossett
Ronald	Bridges	Horn	1953	Saltney
David	Brill	Trombone	1958	Merthyr Tydfil
Adele	Bristow	Oboe	1986	Newport
Heather	Broadbent	Violin	1989	Aberaeron
Gary	Bromage	Cello	1966	Seven Sisters
Basil	Bromham	Oboe	1956	Neath
Helen	Brooks	Flute	1971	Pontypool
Vyvyan	Brooks	Violin	1970	Trelleck
Paul	Broom	Flute	1960	Taff's Well
Stephen	Broom	Viola	1968	Pontypridd
Anthony	Brough	Violin	1973	Conwy
Dorothy	Brown	Viola	1951	Bishopston
George	Brown	Flute	1964	Cardiff
Helen	Brown	Violin	1978	Mountain Ash
David	Bryant	Clarinet	1951	Hawarden
Michael	Brynn	Cello	1960	Cardiff
Henryk	Brzezinka	Viola	1970	Cardiff
Jane	Buckland	Double bass	1982	Treorchy
Richard	Buckley	Percussion	1987	Swansea
Francis	Bucknall	Cello	1978	Monmouth
Juliet	Bucknall	Clarinet	1983	Monmouth
Ruth	Bucknall	Viola	1979	Monmouth
Stephen	Bulfield	Percussion	1979	Rhyl
Victoria	Bulgin	Viola	1968	Penygraig
Felix	Burak	Violin	1970	Penygraig
Helen	Burbidge	Double bass	1981	Pyle
Paul	Burbidge	Double bass	1978	Pyle
Terence	Burke	Violin	1951	Merthyr Tydfil

Steven	Burnard	Violin	1978	Swansea
Susan	Burrows	Cello	1986	Ystrad Mynach
Rachel	Burt	Viola	1986	Aberaeron
Julian	Bush	Bassoon	1962	Carmarthen
Susanna	Büsst	Clarinet	1989	Bangor
Mary	Bute	Viola	1959	Cardiff
Andrew	Byrt	Viola	1979	Aberaeron
Rachel	Byrt	Viola	1985	Aberaeron
Elaine	Cadogan	Violin	1951	Cardiff
Neil	Cadogan	Clarinet	1956	Caerphilly
John	Cale	Viola	1957	Garnant
John	Canter	Violin	1969	Aberdare
Adrian	Carpenter	Cello	1976	Abertillery
Geoffrey	Carpenter	Violin	1964	Pontnewydd
David	Carr	Violin	1975	Newport
Kevin	Catley	Flute	1968	Abercarn
Huw	Ceredig	Clarinet	1966	Aberystwyth
Huw	Ceredig	Percussion	1968	Aberystwyth
Rhodri	Ceredig	Violin	1963	Aberystwyth
Simon	Chalk	Violin	1986	Oakdale
Lewis	Chamberlain	Violin	1960	Barry
Victor	Chamberlain	Violin	1954	Barry
John	Chapman	Cello	1960	Pontypridd
Philip	Chapman	Double bass	1971	Holyhead
Sheila Ann	Chapman	Cello	1958	Marianglas
David	Chappell	Violin	1957	Merthyr Tydfil
Richard	Chapple	Trombone	1953	Swansea
Richard	Charles	Percussion	1988	Caernarfon
Maurice	Checker	Oboe	1952	Newport
Helen Jane	Chefworth	Violin	1990	Wrexham
Lyn	Childs	Oboe	1959	Goodwick
Lester	Christie	Violin	1959	Cardiff
Joel	Clampus	Violin	1952	Neath
Julian	Clapham	Bassoon	1959	Aberystwyth
Janet	Clapton	Violin	1971	Cardiff
Emily	Clark	Cello	1988	Swansea
Katy	Clark	Violin	1984	Swansea
Nicholas	Clark	Violin	1985	Machen
Rhodri	Clark	Viola	1987	Machen
Brian	Clarke	Cello	1969	Gowerton
Emily	Clarke	Cello	1990	Murton
Eric	Clarke	Clarinet	1964	Port Talbot
John P.	Clarke	Violin	1951	Taff's Well
Robert	Clayton	Horn	1958	Beaumaris
Anthony Michael	Cleaton	Double bass	1987	Merthyr Tydfil
Catherine	Clement	Flute	1984	Llanelli
Dominy	Clements	Flute	1984	Newport
Rhian	Clements	Flute	1985	Llanelli
Helen	Clissold	Violin	1985	Cardiff
Joel	Clompus	Violin	1953	Neath
Joanna	Cobb	Cello	1981	Barry
Sarah	Cobb	Violin	1981	Barry
Helen	Cochrane	Violin	1976	Newport
Jeremy	Cody	Tuba	1971	Pontypridd
Robert	Coles	Trumpet	1975	Newport
Joan	Collier	Violin	1961	Pontypridd
Peter	Conibear	Oboe	1958	Killay
Andrew	Connolly	Horn	1979	Bridgend
Irene	Connolly	Oboe	1983	Broughton
Caitlin	Constable	Viola	1986	Penarth
Clare	Constable	Cello	1983	Penarth
Jean	Constable	Percussion	1955	Pencoed
Martin	Conway	Percussion	1978	Aberystwyth
Rosemary	Cook	Violin	1983	Llangollen

Gareth	Cooke	Double bass	1959	Ogmore Vale
Janet	Cooke	Cello	1980	Bridgend
James	Cooper	Tuba	1976	Wrexham
Sandy	Copeland	Double bass	1979	Menai Bridge
April	Copestake	Trumpet	1974	Nefyn
James	Copper	Tuba	1977	Wrexham
Helen	Cormie	Violin	1990	Argoed
Peter	Cosham	Violin	1967	Cardiff
Elizabeth	Cottam	Violin	1982	Cardiff
Matthew	Cottam	Violin	1985	Cardiff
Tanwen	Counsell	Violin	1990	Cardiff
Derek	Cousins	Tuba	1962	Gorseinon
Christopher	Cowie	Oboe	1982	Cardiff
Philip	Cowley	Trombone	1971	Neath
Neil	Cox	Percussion	1970	Llanelli
Susan	Cox	Oboe	1959	Aberystwyth
Stewart	Crawford	Horn	1976	Caldicot
David	Creel	Clarinet	1967	Llanelli
Richard	Creel	Violin	1964	Llanelli
Andrew	Cresci	Tuba	1978	Skewen
N. Williams	Cressey	Viola	1964	Milford Haven
Pamela	Croker	Violin	1961	Porthcawl
Susan	Croot	Violin	1973	Gowerton
David	Cropper	Horn	1954	Buckley
Timothy	Crossland	Violin	1970	Neath
Brian	Crowley	Violin	1959	Hengoed
Bryan	Crowley	Violin	1957	Penpedairheol
Michael	Crump	Viola	1978	Ebbw Vale
Andrew	Cuff	Trumpet	1971	Pontypridd
John	Cullis	Cello	1961	Cwmfelinfach
Theresa Margaret	Cullis	Violin	1958	Cwmfelinfach
Elizabeth	Curson	Violin	1987	Cimla
Jane	Curwen	Cello	1980	Machynlleth
Gordon	Dale	Violin	1954	Presteigne
Adrian	Dall	Cello	1972	Porthcawl
Phillip	Dando	Trombone	1970	Pencoed
Ann	Danher	Violin	1961	Llandegfan
Geraint	Daniel	Percussion	1976	Caernarfon
Nuw	Daniel	Clarinet	1976	Swansea
David	Daniels	Cello	1978	Porthcawl
Gwyn	Daniels	Trombone	1984	Beddau
Carl	Darby	Violin	1975	Porth
Alun	Darbyshire	Oboe	1987	Menai Bridge
Martin	Dare-Edwards	Violin	1975	Swansea
Joanne	Dark	Violin	1961	Cardiff
Jacqueline	Darke	Violin	1966	Swansea
Judith	Davard	Flute	1979	Brynmawr
Elynned	David	Violin	1990	Abercarn
Eryl	David	Double bass	1955	Bridgend
Stephen	David	Cello	1970	Abertillery
Vanessa	David	Violin	1977	Abercarn
Wayne	David	Oboe	1974	Cefn Cribbwr
Wayne	David	Clarinet	1976	Wrexham
Catrin	David-Jones	Violin	1983	St Clears
Anthony	Davie	Horn	1960	Neath
Alan	Davies	Bassoon	1959	Bridgend
Alan	Davies	Cello	1974	Welshpool
Alexa	Davies	Viola	1975	Penarth
Alexander	Davies	Double bass	1989	Newport
Alun J.	Davies	Violin	1959	Ammanford
Andrew	Davies	Violin	1972	Carmarthen
Angharad	Davies	Violin	1988	Aberystwyth
Ann	Davies	Double bass	1951	Pontypool
Ann	Davies	Flute	1958	Neath

Ann	Davies	Double bass	1961	Llandrindod Wells
Ann	Davies	Flute	1967	Bow Street
Arthur	Davies	Cello	1970	Bow Street
B. Mostyn	Davies	Violin	1957	Church Village
Bethan R.	Davies	Violin	1990	Caernarfon
Bethan Rachel	Davies	Violin	1987	Caernarfon
Betsan Elin	Davies	Cello	1987	Newport
Bleddyn	Davies	Violin	1953	Barry
Bleddyn	Davies	Violin	1954	Bargoed
Bleddyn Price	Davies	Violin	1952	Barry
Brian	Davies	Oboe	1952	Maesteg
Catherine	Davies	Cello	1961	Maesteg
Christopher	Davies	Horn	1979	Welshpool
Clive	Davies	Violin	1953	Ystalyfera
Colin	Davies	Trumpet	1975	Guilsfield
D. Ffrangcon	Davies	Cello	1954	Harlech
Dafydd	Davies	Double bass	1984	Aberystwyth
Damian Walford	Davies	Violin	1988	Aberystwyth
David	Davies	Flute	1953	Pontarddulais
David	Davies	Horn	1967	Risca
David W.	Davies	Flute	1952	Pontarddulais
Derek	Davies	Violin	1961	Rogerstone
Derek	Davies	Viola	1964	Rogerstone
Dominique	Davies	Violin	1980	Newport
Eifion	Davies	Double bass	1958	Skewen
Eleri	Davies	Harp	1966	Machynlleth
Eleri	Davies	Harp	1976	Aberystwyth
Elizabeth	Davies	Horn	1964	Cardiff
Gareth	Davies	Percussion	1969	Mold
Gareth	Davies	Percussion	1971	Bangor
Gareth	Davies	Cello	1983	Caernarfon
Gareth Richard Huw	Davies	Cello	1987	Caernarfon
Georgina	Davies	Clarinet	1979	Gowerton
Geraint	Davies	Violin	1964	Corris
Gethin	Davies	Trumpet	1969	Pontypridd
Gillian	Davies	Violin	1961	Llanelli
Goronwy	Davies	Violin	1961	Corris
Goronwy	Davies	Viola	1964	Corris
Haydn	Davies	Cello	1951	Pontarddulais
Haydn	Davies	Horn	1952	Pontarddulais
Haydn W.	Davies	Horn	1953	Pontarddulais
Helen	Davies	Violin	1977	Maesteg
Helen	Davies	Bassoon	1982	Aberystwyth
Helen	Davies	Violin	1985	Cardiff
Helena	Davies	Cello	1954	Pontarddulais
Hilary	Davies	Oboe	1977	Brynmawr
Hugh	Davies	Violin	1969	Pontypridd
Hugh	Davies	Violin	1970	Fishguard
Huw	Davies	Cello	1983	Cardiff
Hywel	Davies	Violin	1969	Pontypridd
Hywel	Davies	Violin	1973	Pwllheli
Hywel	Davies	Viola	1976	Pwllheli
Ian	Davies	Cello	1968	Carmarthen
Ioan	Davies	Viola	1951	Penclawdd
Ioan	Davies	Cello	1967	Carmarthen
Iona	Davies	Violin	1984	Llangollen
Iona Mair	Davies	Violin	1988	Llangollen
J. Martin	Davies	Violin	1959	Pontarddulais
Janet	Davies	Cello	1961	Port Talbot
Janet	Davies	Percussion	1973	Three Crosses
Jason Walford	Davies	Violin	1988	Aberystwyth
Jean	Davies	Double bass	1964	Fochriw
Jeffrey	Davies	Oboe	1957	Neath
Jennifer	Davies	Double bass	1969	Newtown

John	Davies	Violin	1963	Hendy
John	Davies	Trombone	1978	Neath
John	Davies	Viola	1981	Llanelli
John	Davies	Viola	1982	Ammanford
John G.	Davies	Violin	1951	Brynmawr
John Marc	Davies	Viola	1983	Ammanford
John V.	Davies	Violin	1953	Swansea
John Vivian	Davies	Violin	1952	Swansea
Joyce	Davies	Violin	1951	Prestatyn
Julia	Davies	Violin	1980	Ammanford
Julia	Davies	Violin	1981	Llandybïe
Karl	Davies	Violin	1969	Mountain Ash
Katherine	Davies	Violin	1961	Cardiff
Lawrence	Davies	Trumpet	1956	Blaina
Lisa	Davies	Cello	1972	Cardiff
Llinos	Davies	Viola	1976	Llandeilo
Lyn	Davies	Clarinet	1957	Penygraig
Lynne	Davies	Bassoon	1973	Fishguard
Malcolm	Davies	Viola	1971	Caerphilly
Manon	Davies	Violin	1985	Aberystwyth
Margaret	Davies	Cello	1958	Gorseinon
Margaret	Davies	Cello	1967	Newtown
Margaret	Davies	Cello	1969	Mochdre
Mari	Davies	Flute	1961	Cardiff
Marilyn Louise	Davies	Violin	1990	Crymych
Marion	Davies	Cello	1953	Bridgend
Mererid	Davies	Cello	1980	Cardiff
Michael J.	Davies	Cello	1951	Morriston
Mostyn	Davies	Violin	1959	Church Village
Noel	Davies	Violin	1957	Clydach
Owen	Davies	Violin	1961	Cardiff
Paul	Davies	Violin	1961	Pembroke Dock
Paul	Davies	Oboe	1969	Llanelli
Peter	Davies	Horn	1956	Cardiff
Peter	Davies	Cello	1961	Swansea
Peter N.	Davies	Cello	1964	Swansea
Rachel	Davies	Harp	1990	Clydach
Rebecca	Davies	Flute	1986	Aberystwyth
Rhiannon	Davies	Violin	1983	Llangattock
Rhys	Davies	Viola	1967	Llangefni
Robert	Davies	Viola	1961	Merthyr Tydfil
Roger	Davies	Trombone	1958	Cardiff
Ruth	Davies	Violin	1987	Cardiff
Sally	Davies	Violin	1970	Llanelly
Sally	Davies	Violin	1974	Llandeilo
Sian	Davies	Viola	1977	Bryncoch
Sian	Davies	Oboe	1979	Neath
Sophie	Davies	Violin	1988	Marford
Stephen	Davies	Oboe	1989	Swansea
Timothy	Davies	Bassoon	1989	Swansea
Tudor	Davies	Trumpet	1960	Hirwaun
Valerie	Davies	Cello	1951	Neath
Valerie Marion	Davies	Cello	1952	Bridgend
Vanessa	Davies	Viola	1981	Llangollen
Vivian	Davies	Horn	1954	Blaengwynfi
Vivian	Davies	Horn	1959	Port Talbot
Vivian	Davies	Trumpet	1977	Cwmaman
Vivianne	Davies	Percussion	1963	Hendy
W. E.	Davies	Horn	1951	Pontymoile
William Clive	Davies	Violin	1952	Ystalyfera
William Ioan	Davies	Viola	1952	Penclawdd
Wyn	Davies	Violin	1967	Gowerton
Wyn	Davies	Violin	1969	Three Crosses
Cynthia	Davis	Horn	1969	Cardiff

Ian	Dawson	Trombone	1984	Llansanffraid
Charlotte Emmma	Day	Viola	1987	Llangollen
Emma	Day	Viola	1984	Llangollen
Karen	Demmel	Viola	1980	Port Talbot
Albert	Dennis	Double bass	1972	Neath
Alun	Derbyshire	Oboe	1986	Menai Bridge
Mary	Diddams	Viola	1952	Newport
Anne	Diehl	Violin	1960	Swansea
J. S.	Diehl	Violin	1960	Swansea
Alida	Dixon	Cello	1987	Swansea
Clive	Dobbins	Violin	1967	Gorseinon
Philip	Doddridge	Trombone	1982	Neath
Stephen	Donovan	Cello	1979	Newport
Frank R.	Doolan	Violin	1951	Cardiff
David	Dorey	Horn	1971	Cardiff
Sharon	Dorey	Violin	1990	Gorseinon
Rodney	Dorothy	Violin	1971	Newport
Angela Mary	Dove	Violin	1952	Whitchurch
Elizabeth	Dove	Cello	1956	Whitchurch
Michael	Downing	Trumpet	1978	Pontarddulais
Susan	Drake	Harp	1962	Fishguard
Arnold	Dreaper	Horn	1957	Penarth
John Keith	Duncan	Violin	1958	Newport
Elizabeth	Dungey	Double bass	1984	Haverfordwest
Gareth	Dunley	Trombone	1976	Broughton
Margaret	Dunn	Violin	1967	Garnant
Nicki	Dupuy	Double bass	1984	Bangor
Ryth	Durant	Clarinet	1984	Swansea
Alok	Dutt	Violin	1984	Caerphilly
Heather	Dyer	Violin	1958	Blaengarw
Eirian	Dyfri Jones	Harp	1984	Aberystwyth
Kathryn	Dykes	Viola	1990	Abertillery
Adrian	Eales	Violin	1971	Ystrad Mynach
Geoffret	Eales	Horn	1968	Bargoed
Geoffrey	Eales	Horn	1971	Ystrad Mynach
Gillian	East	Double bass	1951	Milford Haven
Peter	East	Viola	1951	Milford Haven
Graham	Eaton	Violin	1971	Flint
Andrew	Eatough	Cello	1982	Lampeter
Robert	Ecket	Bassoon	1985	Neath
Alison	Edwards	Double bass	1978	Machynlleth
Ann	Edwards	Oboe	1954	Ebbw Vale
Ann	Edwards	Violin	1955	Llanfair P. G.
Ann	Edwards	Cello	1961	Gorseinon
Anne	Edwards	Cor anglais	1955	Ebbw Vale
Catherine	Edwards	Flute	1961	Holyhead
Christopher	Edwards	Trumpet	1972	Newtown
Colin G.	Edwards	Cello	1959	Holyhead
Elin	Edwards	Violin	1976	Cardiff
Fiona	Edwards	Double bass	1974	Newtown
Gillian	Edwards	Cello	1980	Dowlais
Hilary	Edwards	Cello	1956	Llandrindod
Iwan	Edwards	Violin	1956	Llanelli
Jane	Edwards	Double bass	1957	Ystradgynlais
Janet	Edwards	Flute	1981	Dinas Powys
Marion	Edwards	Cello	1961	Pontlliw
Martin	Edwards	Violin	1971	Swansea
Nest	Edwards	Cello	1957	Rhuthun
Owain Tudor	Edwards	Bassoon	1957	Llangollen
Philip	Edwards	Clarinet	1971	Buckley
Rebecca	Edwards	Cello	1978	Beaufort
Richard	Edwards	Cello	1956	Llangollen
Richard	Edwards	Cello	1961	Newtown
Robert	Edwards	Clarinet	1970	Buckley

Robert W.	Edwards	Viola	1966	Llanelli
Selyf	Edwards	Violin	1981	Pontarddulais
Thomas Wynne	Edwards	Trombone	1961	Gorseinon
Azhaar	El Saffar	Violin	1976	Llansadwrn
Carwyn	Ellis	Bassoon	1990	Benllech
Gwyn	Ellis	Violin	1956	Holyhead
Gwyn	Ellis	Viola	1957	Dolgellau
Keith	Ellis	Violin	1956	Risca
Michael	Ellis	Bassoon	1962	Port Talbot
Nicola	Ellis	Flute	1984	Caergwrle
John	Ellis Braithwaite	Tuba	1981	Welshpool
Sian	Ellis-Williams	Clarinet	1961	Holyhead
David	Emanuel	Viola	1975	Skewen
Phillip	Emanuel	Flute	1972	Neath
Nigel	Emery	Cello	1964	Cardiff
Hannah	Emesheimer	Cello	1951	Cardiff
Roger	Emm	Violin	1968	Aberdare
Phillip	Emmanuel	Flute	1971	Skewen
Lionel	Erenburg	Clarinet	1951	Cardiff
Joseph	Erianger	Viola	1953	Cardiff
John	Esaias	Oboe	1969	Kenfig Hill
Adrian	Evans	Trumpet	1966	Pontypridd
Alison	Evans	Double bass	1981	Borth
Alun	Evans	Percussion	1984	Abercynon
Alyn Huw	Evans	Percussion	1985	Abercynon
Anna	Evans	Viola	1957	Talybont
Anthony	Evans	Violin	1979	Llandudno
Berian	Evans	Violin	1956	Brynaman
Branwen	Evans	Violin	1987	Aberystwyth
Brian	Evans	Violin	1959	Maerdy
Cai Llewellyn	Evans	Trumpet	1990	Pontarddulais
Catherine	Evans	Violin	1986	Maesteg
Catherine Mary	Evans	Violin	1987	Maesteg
Ceri	Evans	Violin	1964	Pontlliw
Christine	Evans	Violin	1961	Neath
Christopher	Evans	Percussion	1976	Gorseinon
Colin	Evans	Cello	1960	Holyhead
D. Colin	Evans	Double bass	1959	Ammanford
Dale	Evans	Violin	1974	Aberystwyth
Dale	Evans	Violin	1975	Caerphilly
David	Evans	Horn	1960	Llanelli
David G.	Evans	Violin	1963	Amlwch
David G. B.	Evans	Violin	1964	Amlwch
David Lyn	Evans	Violin	1966	Crynant
Elizabeth	Evans	Violin	1961	Ebbw Vale
Emyr Pugh	Evans	Trombone	1986	Aberystwyth
Erica	Evans	Violin	1969	Wrexham
Fay	Evans	Violin	1972	Aberystwyth
Gareth	Evans	Violin	1978	Llandudno
Geraint	Evans	Double bass	1979	Ferndale
Geraint	Evans	Trombone	1982	Aberystwyth
Glyn	Evans	Trumpet	1955	Merthyr Tydfil
Glyn R.	Evans	Violin	1951	Swansea
Goronwy	Evans	Trumpet	1981	Llanrhystud
Gwenfair Nerys Lloyd	Evans	Viola	1987	Bangor
Haldon	Evans	Trumpet	1970	Pontarddulais
Helen	Evans	Viola	1974	Cardiff
Huw	Evans	Horn	1977	Loughor
Huw	Evans	Horn	1980	Machynlleth
Huw	Evans	Horn	1982	Loughor
Hywel	Evans	Violin	1970	Pontypridd
Ian	Evans	Double bass	1971	Wrexham
J. Glynne	Evans	Double bass	1951	Lanelli
Janet	Evans	Violin	1982	Aberystwyth

Jeffrey	Evans	Trombone	1967	Pontarddulais
John	Evans	Bassoon	1970	Carmarthen
John	Evans	Harp	1970	Gorseinon
John	Evans	Percussion	1971	Gorseinon
John P.	Evans	Trombone	1951	Loughor
Karen	Evans	Violin	1974	Three Crosses
Karen	Evans	Violin	1978	Swansea
Katherine	Evans	Cello	1961	Aberkenfig
Katie	Evans	Oboe	1990	Monmouth
Kenvin	Evans	Trumpet	1966	Pontypridd
Laurence	Evans	Trumpet	1953	Ynyshir
Lyn	Evans	Horn	1955	Ammanford
Marilyn	Evans	Double bass	1959	Pontarddulais
Martin	Evans	Violin	1972	Colwyn Bay
Martin	Evans	Trumpet	1990	Cardiff
Mary	Evans	Clarinet	1983	Bangor
Michael	Evans	Cello	1953	Llanelli
Michael	Evans	Percussion	1977	Pontypridd
Michael A.	Evans	Cello	1951	Llanelli
Muriel	Evans	Cello	1953	Ferndale
Myra	Evans	Violin	1957	Llanelli
Neil	Evans	Violin	1978	Swansea
Nigel	Evans	Violin	1982	Burry Port
Non	Evans	Harp	1971	Cardiff
Peter	Evans	Viola	1951	Penclawdd
Rachel	Evans	Violin	1986	Llandegfan
Rhian	Evans	Violin	1989	Tonpentre
Rhodri	Evans	Horn	1988	Aberystwyth
Richard	Evans	Cello	1962	Newtown
Richard	Evans	Bassoon	1967	Loughor
Robert	Evans	Horn	1986	Cardiff
Rosemary	Evans	Violin	1970	Marford
Ruth	Evans	Flute	1979	Crickhowell
Sian	Evans	Oboe	1961	Cardiff
Sianelen	Evans	Flute	1975	Pwllheli
Simon	Evans	Violin	1976	Colwyn Bay
Stuart	Evans	Flute	1973	Ammanford
Susan	Evans	Cello	1961	Cwmbran
Susan	Evans	Cello	1971	Neath
T. Eifion	Evans	Violin	1951	Ystalyfera
Victoria	Evans	Viola	1956	Swansea
Victoria	Evans	Violin	1988	Aberystwyth
Volan	Evans	Trombone	1955	Markham
William	Evans	Violin	1964	Aberystwyth
Wyn Vaughan	Evans	Cello	1961	Bangor
Wynford	Evans	Cello	1964	Bangor
Adrian	Evett	Bassoon	1969	Briton Ferry
Ian	Evett	Viola	1959	Briton Ferry
Edwin	Eyre	Trumpet	1972	Cwmbran
Margaret	Farren	Cello	1964	Cardiff
Elizabeth Ann	Fernee	Violin	1987	Marford
Robert	Ferris	Double bass	1976	Briton Ferry
Margaret	Field	Double bass	1967	North Cornelly
Margaret	Field	Cello	1970	Porthcawl
Lorna	Finney	Double bass	1974	Guilsfield
Colin	Fisher	Trumpet	1964	Wrexham
Lauren Suzanne	Fitches	Violin	1988	Aberystwyth
Jacqueline Nicole	Fletcher	Viola	1989	Marford
Jeremy	Fletcher	Horn	1988	Aberystwyth
Susan	Fletcher	Double bass	1976	Aberhafesp
Ian	Flower	Violin	1983	Aberdare
Peter	Folland	Tuba	1968	Cwmbran
Stephen	Follant	Tuba	1989	Neath
Andrew	Ford	Trombone	1983	Trewern

Stephen	Ford	Flute	1975	Caerphilly
Lucy	Foster	Oboe	1980	Bow Street
Nicholas	Foster	Clarinet	1980	Bow Street
Robert	Fowler	Viola	1986	Caldicot
Judith	Fox	Violin	1987	Monmouth
Ashley	Frampton	Double bass	1981	Cardiff
Alun	Francis	Horn	1960	Troedyrhiw
David	Francis	Cello	1970	Pontlotyn
Jeffrey D.	Francis	Violin	1951	Port Talbot
Jill	Francis	Violin	1979	Pencoed
Jonathan	Francis	Double bass	1969	Pontlotyn
Judith	Francis	Violin	1971	Llanelli
Mary	Francis	Violin	1970	Llanelli
Menna	Francis	Cello	1955	Bridgend
Peter	Francis	Double bass	1963	Llanelli
Philip	Francis	Violin	1954	Port Talbot
Sidonie	Francis	Violin	1960	Llanelli
David	Francis	Double bass	1971	Pontlotyn
Ivor	Franklyn	Trumpet	1957	Ynyshir
Judith	Fransis	Violin	1972	Llanelli
Bethan	Frieze	Violin	1977	Cardiff
Linda	Frost	Oboe	1957	Saundersfoot
Simon	Fullylove	Violin	1984	Porth
Henry	G. Jones	Viola	1953	Abercrave
Anna Catherine	Gambles	Flute	1987	Denbigh
T. Geoffrey	Gambold	Bassoon	1951	Morriston
Julia	Garatt	Viola	1970	Menai Bridge
Stuart	Gardens	Oboe	1989	Connah's Quay
Peter	Gardner	Violin	1964	Brecon
Rachel	Gardner	Viola	1990	Bridgend
Sian Kathryn	Gardner	Oboe	1990	Bridgend
Julia	Garratt	Viola	1971	Menai Bridge
Susan	Garratt	Cello	1968	Menai Bridge
Anthony	Gay	Violin	1967	Cardiff
Nicholas	Gedge	Viola	1985	Brecon
Fiona	George	Bassoon	1979	Haverfordwest
Heather	George	Viola	1956	Swansea
Jason	George	Percussion	1988	Wrexham
Jeffrey	George	Violin	1959	Maesteg
Kenneth E.	George	Flute	1952	Neath
Rhys	Gerallt	Trombone	1989	Borth
Ronald	Gethin	Double bass	1960	Merthyr Tydfil
Howard	Giles	Violin	1964	Cardiff
Roy	Gillard	Violin	1960	Hirwaun
Giulia	Glennon	Cello	1988	Newport
Richard	Golding	Viola	1974	Caerphilly
John	Good	Flute	1967	Port Talbot
Derek	Gooding	Percussion	1960	Cardiff
Meryl	Goodwin	Violin	1974	Aberystwyth
Stephen	Goss	Viola	1981	Swansea
Anthony P.	Gough	Trumpet	1951	Llandrindod Wells
Dafydd	Gough	Trumpet	1982	Skewen
James	Gower	Viola	1990	Newport
Martin	Graff	Percussion	1978	Treforest
Richard Sheridan	Grainger	Double bass	1989	Wrexham
Ian	Grant	Trumpet	1963	Cwmbran
Simon	Gratton	Oboe	1975	Briton Ferry
Gwyneth	Gravelle	Double bass	1961	Pontarddulais
Paul	Green	Bassoon	1968	Newport
David	Gregory	Trombone	1961	Newport
Dewi	Gregory	Flute	1988	Pontardawe
Ann	Griffiths	Harp	1951	Maesteg
Anna	Griffiths	Cello	1984	Llandudno
David	Griffiths	Percussion	1986	Cardiff

Diana	Griffiths	Viola	1957	Neath
Edward	Griffiths	Viola	1954	Caerphilly
Enid	Griffiths	Viola	1954	Ferndale
Euronwy	Griffiths	Viola	1951	Pwllheli
Gwyn	Griffiths	Violin	1961	Merthyr Tydfil
Hannah	Griffiths	Double bass	1986	Cardiff
Helen	Griffiths	Violin	1979	Bridgend
Huw	Griffiths	Oboe	1970	Cardiff
Jane	Griffiths	Violin	1979	Pembroke
Janet	Griffiths	Clarinet	1972	Porth
John	Griffiths	Violin	1960	Flint
Kelvin	Griffiths	Double bass	1978	Pontarddulais
Kevin	Griffiths	Violin	1974	Brecon
Mair	Griffiths	Cello	1982	Cardiff
Mary	Griffiths	Harp	1956	Maesteg
Mary	Griffiths	Cello	1957	Maesteg
Matthew	Griffiths	Bassoon	1988	Bridgend
Michael	Griffiths	Horn	1953	Swansea
Michael	Griffiths	Oboe	1958	Barry
Patricia	Griffiths	Cello	1956	Blaengarw
Patricia	Griffiths	Violin	1970	Cwmbran
Paul	Griffiths	Flute	1955	Bargoed
Peter	Griffiths	Double bass	1970	Clarbeston Road
Raymond	Griffiths	Violin	1956	Llandrindod
Richard	Griffiths	Violin	1978	Cosheston
Sharron	Griffiths	Harp	1990	Aberystwyth
Sheldon	Griffiths	Percussion	1960	Pontypridd
Sian	Griffiths	Violin	1981	Pembroke
Sian Wyn	Griffiths	Double bass	1989	Haverfordwest
Simon	Griffiths	Horn	1982	Bridgend
Simon	Griffiths	Cello	1985	Aberaman
William	Griffiths	Violin	1964	Holyhead
Rachel	Gronow	Double bass	1984	Neath
Richard	Grose	Oboe	1982	Chepstow
Sylvia	Groskop	Violin	1959	Barry
Colin	Gummer	Trombone	1969	Maerdy
Luke Das	Gupta	Trumpet	1988	Bangor
Huw	Gwilym	Double bass	1986	Llansadwrn
Ceredig	Gwynn	Violin	1959	Aberystwyth
Elizabeth	Gwynne-Jones	Violin	1966	Llangefni
Lesley	Gwyther	Violin	1972	Newport
Valerie	H. Davies	Cello	1953	Neath
Glyn	Hale	Percussion	1957	Oakdale
Alan	Hall	Percussion	1959	Newport
Alan B.	Hall	Tuba	1956	Newport
Catrin	Hall	Cello	1977	Bow Street
Heledd	Hall	Violin	1977	Bow Street
Janice	Hall	Viola	1959	Pontypool
William	Hall	Violin	1975	Croesyceiliog
John	Halley	Bassoon	1982	Bridgend
Robin	Hames	Double bass	1977	Newport
Barbara	Hammond	Percussion	1951	Blackwood
Daniel	Hannaby	Trombone	1952	Merthyr Tydfil
Carl	Hanney	Horn	1951	Swansea
Trevor	Hansel	Cello	1973	Swansea
Christine	Harding	Violin	1990	Caerleon
Christopher	Harding	Flute	1983	Cardiff
Jacab	Hardulak	Violin	1961	Monmouth
Enid	Harper	Violin	1957	Holyhead
Owen	Harpwood	Violin	1967	Margam
Emma	Harrhy	Cello	1987	Newport
Anne	Harries	Violin	1970	Llanelli
Anthony	Harries	Viola	1964	Llanelli
Carol	Harries	Harp	1976	Aberystwyth

David	Harries	Violin	1966	Ammanford
David	Harries	Oboe	1972	Nantgaredig
David	Harries	Horn	1979	Cardiff
Derek	Harries	Double bass	1954	Haverfordwest
Gruffydd	Harries	Flute	1970	Neath
Idris	Harries	Clarinet	1983	Newport
Imogen	Harries	Viola	1985	St David's
John	Harries	Viola	1959	Llanelli
John	Harries	Clarinet	1966	Llanelli
Kenneth	Harries	Trumpet	1952	Ammanford
David	Harris	Cello	1952	Ferndale
Dorothy	Harris	Violin	1951	Merthyr Tydfil
Eileen	Harris	Violin	1956	Cardiff
Graham	Harris	Trombone	1974	Neath
Kathleen	Harris	Double bass	1952	Merthyr Tydfil
Lindsey	Harris	Bassoon	1989	Abergavenny
Melba	Harris	Violin	1959	Rhymney
Neil	Harris	Flute	1972	Cilfynydd
Nia	Harris	Cello	1984	Newport
Sali	Harris	Harp	1979	Ynystawe
Kathleen	Harrison	Violin	1972	Tregynon
Mary	Harrison	Violin	1973	Tregynon
Miranda	Harrison	Violin	1951	Tenby
Christopher	Harry	Violin	1977	Skewen
John	Harvey	Cello	1963	Skewen
Thomas	Hasell	Trombone	1960	Ynysybwl
Peter	Haughton	Bassoon	1952	Saltney
Judith	Havard	Flute	1976	Brynmawr
Margaret	Haycock	Viola	1971	Llandrindod Wells
Ian	Hayes	Violin	1973	Newport
Penelope	Hayes	Violin	1954	Swansea
Andrew	Heald	Double bass	1981	Croesyceilog
Alison	Heaney	Violin	1961	Holyhead
Margaret	Heaney	Cello	1966	Holyhead
Simon	Heghoyan	Violin	1987	Rhaeadr
Peter	Hembrough	Violin	1980	Gwernymynydd
John	Hempenstall	Clarinet	1951	Neath
Michael	Henderson	Viola	1974	Tenby
John	Hendy	Trombone	1966	Beddau
Peter	Hendy	Trombone	1975	Beddau
Julia	Henry	Oboe	1974	Aberystwyth
Iestyn	Henson	Viola	1985	Cardiff
Charles	Heppenstall	Violin	1956	Barry
Christopher	Herbert	Violin	1972	Ebbw Vale
Christopher	Herbert	Violin	1974	Beaufort
David	Herbert	Tuba	1975	Welshpool
Trevor	Herbert	Trombone	1962	Treorchy
Peter	Heron	Clarinet	1981	Cardiff
Sian	Hewitt	Bassoon	1983	Buckley
Susan	Hewitt	Flute	1975	Brecon
Roselle	Hewlett	Cello	1959	Pontypool
Sylvia	Hewlett	Viola	1961	Pontypool
Kenneth	Hewlings	Celesta	1953	Tenby
Hazel	Hibbert	Violin	1961	Pontypool
Carol	Hickey	Viola	1954	Merthyr Tydfil
Philip	Hier	Cello	1966	Pyle
Julie	Higgins	Violin	1980	Cardiff
Alan	Higham	Clarinet	1960	Cardiff
Eleri	Highes	Violin	1981	Pwllheli
Julian	Highson	Violin	1961	Neath
Rachel Louise	Hiley	Violin	1988	Crickhowell
Christopher	Hill	Cello	1973	Penally
John Lyndon	Hill	Trumpet	1962	Pontypridd
Jonathan	Hill	Oboe	1975	Caldicot

Lisa	Hill	Clarinet	1988	Gowerton
Marion	Hill	Violin	1973	Penally
Michael	Hill	Trumpet	1952	Merthyr Tydfil
David	Hillier	Violin	1981	Blackwood
Ruth	Hills	Violin	1982	Cardiff
Rachel	Himbury	Violin	1987	Cardiff
Nigel	Hiscock	Horn	1978	Swansea
Naomi Anne	Hitchings	Violin	1987	Bridgend
Jennifer	Hobday	Violin	1961	Llanelli
Caryn	Hockings	Violin	1975	Cardiff
Kenneth	Hodge	Percussion	1963	Llanelli
Cecily	Holliday	Violin	1951	Port Talbot
Phyllis	Hollington	Trumpet	1960	Rhiwabon
Clayton	Hollins	Percussion	1980	Buckley
Richard	Hood	Trumpet	1977	Ogmore-by-Sea
Ann	Hooley	Violin	1966	Merthyr Tydfil
Sean	Hooper	Percussion	1968	Briton Ferry
Eirian	Hopcyn	Cello	1964	Llandysul
Byron	Hopkin	Horn	1990	Cardiff
Elinor	Hopkin	Cello	1987	Aberystwyth
Gerald	Hopkin	Violin	1973	Penygraig
Alun	Hopkins	Clarinet	1969	Skewen
Brian	Hopkins	Violin	1959	Pontarddulais
David	Hopkins	Clarinet	1968	Gorseinon
David Brian	Hopkins	Violin	1960	Pontarddulais
Janet	Hopkins	Viola	1961	Killay
Judith	Hopkins	Cello	1958	Killay
Keith	Hopkins	Cello	1961	Rhosili
Stuart	Hopkins	Trumpet	1988	Aberaman
James	Hopper	Violin	1986	Aberystwyth
John	Hopper	Trombone	1989	Aberystwyth
Stephen	Howell	Cello	1969	Gowerton
Dorothy	Howells	Violin	1959	Blaenafon
Huw	Howells	Double bass	1955	Gorseinon
Mark	Howells	Oboe	1973	Neath
Enid	Howlett	Viola	1972	Pontypool
Richard	Hudson	Violin	1976	Kilgetty
Alan	Hugh	Cello	1951	Penygraig
Siriol	Hugh-Jones	Cello	1984	Mountain Ash
Alan	Hughes	Horn	1954	Gorseinon
Carys	Hughes	Harp	1981	Denbigh
Catrin Anne	Hughes	Clarinet	1990	Llanelli
Ceri Wyn	Hughes	Violin	1960	Llangefni
Dafydd	Hughes	Oboe	1984	Northop Hall
David	Hughes	Horn	1963	Porthcawl
David Rhys	Hughes	Viola	1960	Ynysybwl
Eleri	Hughes	Violin	1979	Pwllheli
Huw	Hughes	Bassoon	1980	Machynlleth
Jayne	Hughes	Violin	1985	Cardiff
John Martin	Hughes	Cello	1961	Llangefni
Mansel	Hughes	Violin	1959	Swansea
Marilyn	Hughes	Oboe	1967	Newtown
Meilyr	Hughes	Trumpet	1960	Llanelli
Menai	Hughes	Harp	1959	Penrhyndeudraeth
Nigel	Hughes	Trombone	1989	Broughton
Robert	Hughes	Trombone	1973	Welshpool
Rosemarie	Hughes	Cello	1969	Cardiff
Catherine	Hughes-Jones	Violin	1961	Church Village
Julian	Hughson	Violin	1962	Neath
Alwyn	Humphreys	Viola	1961	Bodffordd
Bwynfor	Humphreys	Violin	1961	Llandudno
David Wyn	Humphreys	Violin	1960	Gaerwen
Gwynfor	Humphreys	Violin	1962	Llandudno
Joanne	Humphreys	Violin	1989	Trelewis

Margaret R.	Humphreys	Harp	1951	Waenfawr
Patricia	Humphries	Violin	1959	Tredegar
Kenneth	Hunt	Violin	1974	Newport
Ann	Hunter	Clarinet	1960	Cardiff
Joyce	Hunter	Oboe	1961	Colwyn Bay
Mary	Hunter	Oboe	1951	Swansea
Jon	Hutchings	Percussion	1972	Abertillery
Rhodri	Huw	Tuba	1989	Talybont
Mary	Inglesant	Cello	1970	Kenfig Hill
David	Ingram	Violin	1984	Cardiff
Anthony	Isaac	Oboe	1956	Port Talbot
Abigail	Jackson	Cello	1989	Crickhowell
Jeremy	Jackson	Violin	1990	Newtown
Julian	Jackson	Violin	1982	Newtown
Simon	Jackson	Violin	1979	Newtown
Stephen	Jackson	Horn	1983	Cardif
Penny	Jacobs	Clarinet	1982	Swansea
Daphne	Jago	Violin	1951	Neath
Alyn	James	Trumpet	1977	Cwmgwrach
Aneuryn L.	James	Trombone	1959	Trefor
Bethan	James	Violin	1982	Aberystwyth
Darrel	James	Trumpet	1979	Ystalyfera
Gareth	James	Viola	1971	Pontycymer
Gwenno Mair	James	Violin	1987	Aberystwyth
Huw	James	Trumpet	1975	Tonna
Huw	James	Violin	1985	Aberdare
Hywel	James	Oboe	1975	Holyhead
Ian M.	James	Viola	1952	Gowerton
Jeremy Glyn	James	Viola	1986	Llanferres
Linda	James	Viola	1972	Abertillery
Lynn	James	Violin	1953	Swansea
Marjory	James	Viola	1953	Swansea
Mary	James	Viola	1964	Pembroke Dock
Mary Ruth	James	Viola	1960	Pembroke Dock
Nigel	James	Violin	1966	Penclawdd
Peter	James	Double bass	1955	Swansea
Richard	James	Trumpet	1974	Tonna
Robert	James	Violin	1974	Trearddur Bay
Ronald	James	Double bass	1957	Ferndale
Ruth	James	Clarinet	1972	Cardiff
Shelia	James	Viola	1977	Fforestfach
Thomas Lloyd	James	Violin	1958	Pembroke Dock
Wendy	Jane Kemp	Cello	1986	Holyhead
Gareth	Jay	Viola	1955	Briton Ferry
John	Jeffery	Percussion	1967	Ferndale
David John	Jeffreys	Violin	1989	Pencoed
Aelwen	Jenkins	Percussion	1978	Llantrisant
Alison	Jenkins	Violin	1984	Loughor
Alistair	Jenkins	Viola	1990	Swansea
Andrew	Jenkins	Trombone	1967	Llanelli
Anthony	Jenkins	Viola	1963	Newtown
Anthony	Jenkins	Violin	1971	Carmarthen
Bronwen	Jenkins	Flute	1961	Cardiff
Bryan	Jenkins	Cello	1980	Ynyshir
Byron	Jenkins	Horn	1974	Llanelli
Clare	Jenkins	Cello	1984	Cardigan
Cyril	Jenkins	Violin	1952	Ystradgynlais
Elizabeth	Jenkins	Viola	1958	Blaengwynfi
Ffion	Jenkins	Clarinet	1986	Cardiff
Huw	Jenkins	Horn	1970	Skewen
John	Jenkins	Trumpet	1959	Skewen
Karin	Jenkins	Violin	1984	Briton Ferry
Karl	Jenkins	Oboe	1960	Penclawdd
Llinos	Jenkins	Violin	1963	Dolgellau

Margaret	Jenkins	Violin	1961	Swansea
Mark	Jenkins	Double bass	1983	Briton Ferry
Michael	Jenkins	Tuba	1958	Gurnos
Nia Keinor	Jenkins	Harp	1987	Swansea
Paul	Jenkins	Double bass	1967	Port Talbot
Paul	Jenkins	Violin	1969	Newtown
Paul	Jenkins	Cello	1970	Port Talbot
Paul	Jenkins	Viola	1972	Newtown
Paul	Jenkins	Violin	1976	Carmarthen
Peter	Jenkins	Violin	1977	Carmarthen
Sian	Jenkins	Viola	1983	Carmarthen
Stephen	Jenkins	Double bass	1979	Cardigan
Gareth	Jenkinson	Violin	1974	Pyle
Cathryn	John	Viola	1976	Porthcawl
Delyth	John	Viola	1982	Merthyr Tydfil
Edward	John	Trumpet	1986	Swansea
Gareth	John	Violin	1968	Pontllanfraith
Gareth	John	Cello	1971	Llanrhystud
Geraint	John	Cello	1951	Gowerton
Haydn	John	Horn	1952	Cardiff
Kevin	John	Viola	1978	Aberystwyth
Pauline	John	Double bass	1974	Gowerton
Stephen	John	Violin	1972	Merthyr Tydfil
Terence	Johns	Horn	1961	Hirwaun
Ellen	Johnson	Cello	1981	Llanferres
Helen	Johnson	Viola	1968	Newport
Tom	Johnston	Double bass	1990	Crickhowell
Jane	Jonathon	Cello	1961	Abergavenny
Alan	Jones	Horn	1959	Cardiff
Alan	Jones	Trombone	1963	Carmarthen
Alan	Jones	Horn	1967	Welshpool
Alice	Jones	Bassoon	1961	Pontypool
Allen	Jones	Violin	1961	Port Talbot
Alun	Jones	Percussion	1955	Blackwood
Alun	Jones	Horn	1957	Cardiff
Alun S.	Jones	Viola	1956	Gorseinon
Amanda	Jones	Harp	1973	Swansea
Andrew	Jones	Trumpet	1978	Buckley
Andrew	Jones	Viola	1979	Ammanford
Andrew	Jones	Trumpet	1984	Kidwelly
Andrew	Jones	Trombone	1988	Blaenafon
Andrew	Jones	Tuba	1990	Sketty
Angela	Jones	Trumpet	1970	Ammanford
Angharad	Jones	Violin	1986	Bala
Ann	Jones	Violin	1975	Llanelli
Anthony	Jones	Violin	1970	Carmarthen
Arfona	Jones	Violin	1951	Ponciau
Arwyn	Jones	Cello	1974	Pyle
Barrie W.	Jones	Violin	1957	Llanbradach
Benjamin	Jones	Horn	1988	Cardiff
Beth	Jones	Bassoon	1956	Oakdale
Bethan	Jones	Violin	1964	Newport
Bethan	Jones	Violin	1969	Caersws
Bethan Elfed	Jones	Bassoon	1988	Benllech
Brian	Jones	Violin	1951	Rhiwabon
Brian	Jones	Double bass	1961	Welshpool
Bryan	Jones	Violin	1976	Port Talbot
Carys	Jones	Viola	1961	Brynsiencyn
Carys Lloyd	Jones	Violin	1959	Wrexham
Catherine	Jones	Bassoon	1972	Abergavenny
Catrin	Jones	Violin	1982	St Clears
Catrin Morris	Jones	Harp	1987	Menai Bridge
Celia	Jones	Violin	1963	Newtown
Ceri Wynne	Jones	Viola	1987	Aberystwyth

Charlotte	Jones	Cello	1989	Swansea
Christina	Jones	Violin	1961	Swansea
Christine	Jones	Violin	1979	Welshpool
Christopher	Jones	Bassoon	1979	Aberystwyth
Claire	Jones	Viola	1976	Bow Street
Clive	Jones	Flute	1963	Llanidloes
D. Alan	Jones	Horn	1968	Welshpool
D. Arwyn	Jones	Violin	1951	Ammanford
D. Theodore	Jones	Oboe	1968	Caersws
David	Jones	Oboe	1968	Hendy
David	Jones	Viola	1978	Port Talbot
David E.	Jones	Violin	1964	Llangefni
David G.	Jones	Bassoon	1959	Tredegar
David Rayner	Jones	Cor anglais	1961	Briton Ferry
David T.	Jones	Oboe	1963	Caersws
Dennis Rowland	Jones	Double bass	1959	Llanelli
Derek	Jones	Violin	1980	Swansea
Dewi	Jones	Horn	1969	Pwllheli
Dylan Llŷr	Jones	Violin	1989	Bala
Edward	Jones	Trombone	1987	Penmaen-mawr
Eifion	Jones	Violin	1984	Resolfen
Eira	Jones	Harp	1979	Aberystwyth
Eirian Dyfri	Jones	Harp	1987	Aberystwyth
Eleanor	Jones	Violin	1983	Brecon
Elizabeth	Jones	Violin	1961	Brynsiencyn
Ellen	Jones	Double bass	1983	Treorchy
Elsbeth	Jones	Harp	1964	Aberystwyth
Emrys	Jones	Percussion	1963	Newtown
Emyr	Jones	Horn	1975	Llandudno
Endaf Emlyn	Jones	Violin	1959	Pwllheli
Eric	Jones	Trumpet	1953	Loughor
Erith	Jones	Trumpet	1961	Glanaman
Eulanwy	Jones	Cello	1957	Lampeter
Eurgain	Jones	Percussion	1961	Llanelli
Felicity	Jones	Violin	1990	Monmouth
Fleur	Jones	Violin	1956	Denbigh
Florence	Jones	Double bass	1959	Cwmbran
Gareth	Jones	Cello	1951	Blaina
Gareth	Jones	Violin	1954	Nantymoel
Gareth	Jones	Tuba	1963	Llanelli
Gareth	Jones	Violin	1970	Pyle
Gareth	Jones	Viola	1977	Port Talbot
Geraint	Jones	Trumpet	1973	Maesteg
Gethin	Jones	Cello	1978	Pontardawe
Glyn	Jones	Trumpet	1959	Cwmbran
Glyn Aelwyn	Jones	Oboe	1988	Aberystwyth
Grace	Jones	Violin	1951	Pontllanfraith
Graham	Jones	Viola	1951	Aberdare
Gwawr	Jones	Viola	1961	Neath
Gwilym Aethwy	Jones	Double bass	1988	Menai Bridge
Gwyn	Jones	Violin	1978	Welshpool
Gwyn Cadfan	Jones	Cello	1958	Blaenau Ffestiniog
Helen	Jones	Violin	1977	Llanelli
Helen Wynn	Jones	Violin	1983	Llandeilo
Helene	Jones	Flute	1957	Cardiff
Henry G. A.	Jones	Viola	1951	Abercrave
Hilary	Jones	Oboe	1963	Merthyr Tydfil
Hilary	Jones	Flute	1978	Ystrad Mynach
Howard	Jones	Trumpet	1976	Tredegar
Huw	Jones	Violin	1971	Rhuthun
Hywel	Jones	Violin	1961	Blaenau Ffestiniog
Hywel	Jones	Violin	1962	Welshpool
Hywel	Jones	Violin	1976	Fishguard
Hywel	Jones	Viola	1977	Port Talbot

Ian	Jones	Double bass	1967	Caersws
Ian	Jones	Clarinet	1981	Wrexham
Ieuan	Jones	Trombone	1977	Rhuthun
Ieuan	Jones	Harp	1977	Meifod
Isobell	Jones	Violin	1984	Porthcawl
Iwan	Jones	Violin	1977	Amlwch
J. Arwyn	Jones	Cello	1952	Pwllheli
J. Ashton	Jones	Clarinet	1956	Arthog
J. Clifford	Jones	Trombone	1954	Ystalyfera
J. Hugh	Jones	Tuba	1963	Bridgend
J. Malcolm	Jones	Violin	1954	Cardiff
Jacqueline	Jones	Flute	1979	Port Talbot
John	Jones	Violin	1953	Merthyr Tudfil
John	Jones	Horn	1960	Clydach
John	Jones	Cello	1969	Wrexham
John H.	Jones	Tuba	1964	Bridgend
John R.	Jones	Violin	1951	Blackwood
John V.	Jones	Horn	1959	Clydach
Julie	Jones	Horn	1986	Dinas Powys
Juliet	Jones	Violin	1978	Caerphilly
Keith	Jones	Flute	1951	Hawarden
Kevin	Jones	Horn	1984	Port Talbot
Leighton	Jones	Horn	1963	Felinfoel
Lilwen	Jones	Violin	1952	Pwllheli
Malcolm	Jones	Violin	1955	Cardiff
Mari	Jones	Violin	1957	Machynlleth
Mari	Jones	Violin	1959	Llandudno
Marian	Jones	Violin	1962	Blaenau Ffestiniog
Marianne	Jones	Viola	1956	Brecon
Maurice	Jones	Trombone	1963	Risca
Meryl	Jones	Percussion	1981	Aberystwyth
Meryl Wyn	Jones	Percussion	1982	Treorchy
Michael	Jones	Bassoon	1964	Newtown
Michael	Jones	Violin	1984	Wrexham
Mona	Jones	Harp	1967	Ffestiniog
Nerys-Ann	Jones	Oboe	1977	Bow Street
Nicholas	Jones	Bassoon	1980	Swansea
Noreen	Jones	Violin	1955	Ferndale
Norman McLeod	Jones	Clarinet	1963	Cardiff
Olwen	Jones	Violin	1966	Machynlleth
Olwen	Jones	Viola	1988	Penisa'r-waun
Patricia	Jones	Percussion	1979	North Cornelly
Paul	Jones	Trumpet	1988	Bridgend
Paul Francis	Jones	Percussion	1989	Mold
Paula	Jones	Clarinet	1985	Builth Wells
Peter	Jones	Violin	1970	Caerphilly
Peter	Jones	Double bass	1976	Cwmbran
Peter	Jones	Violin	1982	Caerphilly
Peter	Jones	Horn	1983	Port Talbot
Peter Elias	Jones	Violin	1958	Llangefni
Philip	Jones	Clarinet	1968	Wrexham
Philip	Jones	Oboe	1971	Wrexham
Philip	Jones	Bassoon	1977	Tondu
Philippa	Jones	Oboe	1963	Abergavenny
Rachel	Jones	Viola	1990	Cilfrew
Rebecca	Jones	Bassoon	1982	Llanelli
Rebecca	Jones	Violin	1986	Neath
Rebecca	Jones	Harp	1989	Maesteg
Rene Ellis	Jones	Viola	1951	Pwllheli
Rhian	Jones	Violin	1970	Holyhead
Rhian	Jones	Oboe	1977	Aberystwyth
Rhian Lloyd	Jones	Oboe	1985	Cardiff
Rhian Louise	Jones	Viola	1988	Cimla
Rhiannon Lloyd	Jones	Oboe	1988	Cardiff

Rhodri	Jones	Horn	1987	Cowbridge
Rhodri Wynn	Jones	Oboe	1983	Aberystwyth
Rhys Gerallt	Jones	Trombone	1986	Borth
Robert	Jones	Tuba	1972	Prestatyn
Ruth	Jones	Horn	1979	Cardiff
Sandra	Jones	Viola	1964	Cardiff
Shirley	Jones	Violin	1952	Aberdare
Sian	Jones	Cello	1988	Aberystwyth
Sian Evelyn	Jones	Violin	1987	Mountain Ash
Sioned	Jones	Harp	1964	Newtown
Siwan	Jones	Harp	1974	Cardiff
Stephen	Jones	Horn	1970	Cardiff
Steven	Jones	Violin	1975	Brecon
Stuart	Jones	Bassoon	1963	Usk
Susan	Jones	Clarinet	1966	Llanbedrog
Susan	Jones	Violin	1968	Glynneath
Susan	Jones	Violin	1977	Llanfyllin
Timothy	Jones	Viola	1984	Caerphilly
Timothy	Jones	Violin	1985	Penygraig
Tudor	Jones	Cello	1952	Ystradgynlais
Veronica	Jones	Violin	1968	Cardiff
William	Jones	Tuba	1966	Llangefni
William Roger	Jones	Clarinet	1959	Abersoch
Wynford	Jones	Horn	1964	Pontypridd
Heather	Joseph	Viola	1956	Machen
Anthony	Josty	Bassoon	1957	Cardiff
Stuart	Kale	Double bass	1961	Skewen
Bernard	Kane	Viola	1990	Cardiff
Catherine	Kearns	Violin	1955	Denbigh
Sally	Kearns	Viola	1952	Denbigh
Francis	Kelleher	Clarinet	1954	Cardiff
Wendy	Kemp	Cello	1985	Holyhead
Corinne	Kent	Viola	1976	Caerphilly
Philip	Kerby	Trumpet	1987	Cardiff
Margaret	Kerr	Double bass	1954	Cross Keys
Gareth	Key	Trombone	1973	Aberdare
John	Key	Trumpet	1964	Cwmbran
David	Kift	Trombone	1959	Pontardawe
Nigel	Kift	Trombone	1960	Pontardawe
Richard John Ll.	Killen	Tuba	1990	Cardiff
Anjela	King	Violin	1983	Rhyl
Martin	King	Percussion	1990	Cardiff
Terence	King	Trumpet	1961	Ammanford
Donald	Knight	Violin	1953	Ystradgynlais
Julia	Knight	Cello	1956	Denbigh
Ann	Kreischer	Cello	1953	Skewen
Helen	Lacey	Cello	1984	Bridgend
Jacqueline	Lake	Double bass	1986	Neath
Peter	Lamb	Double bass	1963	Haverfordwest
Lloyd	Landry	Trumpet	1956	Ystalyfera
Andrew	Lane	Flute	1973	Abergele
David	Langford	Tuba	1972	Neath
Gwyn	Langham	Violin	1959	Pontypridd
Mark Andrew	Lansom	Violin	1988	Wrexham
David	Laviers	Viola	1967	Newtown
Betsy	Law	Viola	1951	Monmouth
Susan	Leach	Violin	1969	Newtown
Nigel	Leadbeater	Trombone	1975	Kidwelly
Bleddyn	Lear	Violin	1963	Bridgend
Douglas	Lear	Oboe	1966	Porthcawl
Hai Ying	Lee	Violin	1989	Wrexham
Geoffrey	Leigh	Violin	1957	Cardiff
Juliet	Leighton-Jones	Violin	1981	Caerphilly
Alan D.	Lewis	Clarinet	1963	Cardiff

Brian	Lewis	Double bass	1959	Newport
Catrin Mair	Lewis	Viola	1989	Mold
Cecilie	Lewis	Violin	1951	Hakin
Christopher Robert	Lewis	Trumpet	1987	Tenby
D. Geraint	Lewis	Violin	1964	Pontpridd
Darryl	Lewis	Cello	1980	Neath
David	Lewis	Horn	1975	Neath
David G.	Lewis	Viola	1958	Maesteg
David Geraint	Lewis	Violin	1961	Pontypridd
Eleanor	Lewis	Viola	1982	Neath
Eric	Lewis	Violin	1959	Gorseinon
Esme	Lewis	Flute	1954	Nantyglo
G. Moira	Lewis	Violin	1964	Goodwick
Gareth	Lewis	Viola	1959	Maesteg
Geraint	Lewis	Violin	1963	Pontypridd
Gloria	Lewis	Double bass	1960	Merthyr Tydfil
Glynis	Lewis	Violin	1967	Cardiff
Gwenda	Lewis	Clarinet	1956	Aberystwyth
Gwilym	Lewis	Viola	1957	Holyhead
Heather	Lewis	Violin	1957	Neath
Hywel	Lewis	Trombone	1972	Machynlleth
Jane	Lewis	Viola	1960	Maesteg
Jayne	Lewis	Viola	1985	Aberaeron
Joan	Lewis	Cello	1951	Hakin
Joan	Lewis	Cello	1954	Milford Haven
John	Lewis	Trombone	1954	Cardiff
John W.	Lewis	Viola	1956	Llanelli
Keith	Lewis	Cello	1963	Llangennech
Kenneth	Lewis	Trumpet	1961	Cwm
Margaret	Lewis	Cello	1970	Abertillery
Michael	Lewis	Viola	1961	Maesteg
Moira	Lewis	Violin	1966	Goodwick
Noel A.	Lewis	Violin	1951	Ammanford
Pamela	Lewis	Viola	1951	Hakin
Patricia	Lewis	Viola	1951	Hakin
Rachel	Lewis	Violin	1972	Goodwick
Raye	Lewis	Cello	1960	Cardiff
Richard	Lewis	Double bass	1972	Newtown
Richard	Lewis	Horn	1990	Sketty
Richard Eifion	Lewis	Trumpet	1987	Newport
Roger	Lewis	Cello	1964	Carmarthen
Roger	Lewis	Horn	1971	Bridgend
Ruth	Lewis	Violin	1961	Rhosmeirch
Terry	Lewis	Violin	1952	Merthyr Tydfil
Thomas	Lewis	Flute	1951	Newport
David	Lexton	Violin	1961	Cardiff
Robert	Leyshon	Violin	1980	Bangor
Malu	Lin	Violin	1981	Aberystwyth
Anne	Lindsay	Cello	1956	Merthyr Tydfil
Diana	Llewellyn	Cello	1969	Port Talbot
Grant	Llewellyn	Cello	1972	Saundersfoot
Huw	Llewellyn	Trombone	1980	Penarth
Paul	Llewellyn	Cello	1951	Swansea
David	Llewellyn - Jones	Clarinet	1959	Swansea
Paul	Llewelyn	Tuba	1953	Swansea
Mary	Llewhellin	Violin	1952	Hakin
Aled	Lloyd	Double bass	1986	Aberystwyth
Amanda	Lloyd	Violin	1990	Gorseinon
Anthony	Lloyd	Percussion	1971	Newtown
David	Lloyd	Violin	1963	Cornelly
Eirion Wyn	Lloyd	Violin	1952	Trebanos
Elinor	Lloyd	Cello	1975	Cardiff
Gareth	Lloyd	Double bass	1989	Aberfan
Gaynor	Lloyd	Violin	1988	Aberystwyth

Gerald	Lloyd	Violin	1956	Swansea
Glyn	Lloyd	Trombone	1958	Tonyrefail
Huw	Lloyd	Violin	1966	Neath
Huw	Lloyd	Bassoon	1990	Cardiff
Jeffrey	Lloyd	Violin	1956	Bryncethin
Jenny	Lloyd	Cello	1988	Cardiff
Joanne	Lloyd	Violin	1985	Wrexham
Margaret	Lloyd	Viola	1961	Caersws
Marion	Lloyd	Viola	1952	Neath
Meinir	Lloyd	Harp	1962	Rhuthun
Morfudd	Lloyd	Harp	1951	Rhuthun
Nerys Hâf	Lloyd	Harp	1988	Aberystwyth
Sarah	Lloyd	Flute	1979	Ogmore-by-Sea
Teifi	Lloyd	Double bass	1964	Ferndale
Gwerfyl Nerys	Lloyd Evans	Viola	1986	Bangor
Ceri	Lloyd Jones	Violin	1982	Cardiff
Owen	Lloyd-Evans	Double bass	1984	Bangor
Ruth	Lloyd-Jones	Horn	1978	Cardiff
Rosemary	Lock	Flute	1981	Cardiff
Martyn	Locke	Bassoon	1976	Neath
Alan	Lockyer	Horn	1973	Neath
Peter	Lodwick	Cello	1960	Neath
Andrew	Lounds	Trumpet	1967	Severn Sisters
Clive	Lowman	Viola	1976	Newport
Jeanette	Lucas	Oboe	1984	Aberystwyth
Wendy	Lucas	Violin	1984	Aberystwyth
Euros	Lyn	Trombone	1989	Swansea
Ian	Lynch	Trumpet	1982	Northop
Gerald	MacPherson	Cello	1951	Swansea
Hilary	Maggs	Oboe	1977	Monmouth
Sian	Maggs	Viola	1975	Newport
Kate	Magnay	Flute	1990	Cowbridge
David R.	Mallett	Trumpet	1963	Pontnewydd
Valerie	Mallett	Horn	1951	Cardiff
Kenneth	Manning	Clarinet	1963	Maesteg
Trevor	Maplestone	Violin	1985	Cwmbrân
Hugh	Marchant	Percussion	1966	Caersws
Anne-Marie	Marks	Violin	1968	Llanelli
Robert	Marks	Clarinet	1974	Llanelli
Richard	Marshall	Viola	1981	Bangor
Aled Tudor	Marshman	Viola	1986	Wrexham
Caroline	Marshman	Cello	1977	Pontypridd
Anthony	Marston	Bassoon	1987	Caernarfon
Andrew	Martin	Viola	1986	Cardiff
Kenneth	Martin	Violin	1979	Bangor
Richard	Martin	Viola	1980	Bangor
Richard	Martyn	Horn	1966	Taff's Well
Dylan	Marvelly	Double bass	1988	Milford Haven
A. Towyn	Mason	Violin	1952	Tenby
Emily	Mason	Violin	1954	Swansea
Helen F.	Mason	Viola	1951	Swansea
Sarah	Mason	Flute	1983	Neath
Towyn A.	Mason	Violin	1951	Tenby
Edwin	Massey	Bassoon	1984	Penarth
Claire	Masterton	Violin	1989	Caerleon
Errol	Matthers	Violin	1966	Barry
Iris	McCanch	Violin	1970	Haverfordwest
Kevin	McCarry	Violin	1978	Swansea
David	McElvay	Violin	1978	Williamstown
John	McGivan	Viola	1960	Swansea
Ceri	McInally	Tuba	1988	Pembroke
Sian	McInally	Violin	1985	Pembroke
David	McKelvay	Violin	1977	Williamstown
George	McLean	Viola	1956	Pembroke Dock

Alan	Meade	Viola	1966	Bridgend
Daviel	Meade	Tuba	1969	Glynneath
Gwenan	Meirion	Harp	1957	Bala
Christopher	Melin	Violin	1986	Pontardawe
David	Mendus	Oboe	1959	Swansea
Gordon	Mepham	Violin	1955	Barry
Jennifer	Meredith	Violin	1960	Brecon
Margaret	Meredith	Violin	1961	Pontypirdd
Rachel	Meredith	Violin	1977	Abergavenny
Stephen	Merriman	Clarinet	1979	Haverfordwest
Bethan	Miles	Viola	1963	Aberystwyth
Dafydd	Miles	Cello	1961	Aberystwyth
Gruffydd	Miles	Cello	1959	Aberystwyth
Sian	Miles	Double bass	1969	Haverfordwest
Anthony	Miller	Trombone	1959	Rhoose
D. Anderson	Miller	Horn	1955	Prestatyn
Jacquetta	Miller	Violin	1951	Hakin
Peter	Mills	Trombone	1966	Colwyn Bay
Alan	Milosevic	Violin	1971	Port Talbot
Donald	Mogford	Violin	1951	Pontarddulais
Robert	Molcher	Horn	1951	Cardiff
Barbara	Moore	Violin	1951	Abertillery
Adele	Morgan	Bassoon	1983	Swansea
Ann	Morgan	Harp	1969	Cardiff
Deiniol	Morgan	Tuba	1988	Aberystwyth
Delyth	Morgan	Harp	1963	Aberystwyth
Eirian	Morgan	Harp	1959	Barmouth
Gregory	Morgan	Trombone	1976	Treorchy
Heulwen	Morgan	Viola	1957	Argoed
Huw	Morgan	Violin	1990	Llanbrynmair
Janet	Morgan	Clarinet	1969	Builth Wells
Janet	Morgan	Oboe	1971	Builth Wells
Jeannine	Morgan	Violin	1988	Swansea
John	Morgan	Trumpet	1974	Llanelli
Jonathan	Morgan	Percussion	1980	Treorchy
Judith	Morgan	Harp	1954	Cardiff
Judith	Morgan	Viola	1972	Builth Wells
Kenneth	Morgan	Violin	1951	Carmarthen
Kenneth	Morgan	Bassoon	1951	Gowerton
Kevin	Morgan	Tuba	1977	Treorchy
Lyn	Morgan	Violin	1985	Gowerton
Owen	Morgan	Violin	1984	Swansea
Peter	Morgan	Bassoon	1966	Neath
Philip	Morgan	Violin	1968	Briton Ferry
Rachel	Morgan	Harp	1968	Cardiff
Richard	Morgan	Oboe	1953	Tredegar
Simon	Morgan	Horn	1981	Bridgend
Wyn	Morgan	Double bass	1976	Aberystwyth
Reynell	Moris	Horn	1964	Newtown
Jane	Morrell	Flute	1981	Bangor
Anne	Morris	Cello	1951	Llansteffan
Catherine	Morris	Oboe	1989	Monmouth
D. Roland	Morris	Double bass	1954	Llanelli
Daniel	Morris	Violin	1961	Portmadoc
Elen	Morris	Flute	1963	Rhosllannerchrugog
Emsyl	Morris	Violin	1964	Portmadoc
Geraint	Morris	Violin	1983	Neath
Hilary	Morris	Viola	1960	Blaenau Ffestiniog
Katherine	Morris	Oboe	1988	Monmouth
Keith	Morris	Percussion	1959	Port Talbot
Keith	Morris	Percussion	1985	Bangor
Paul	Morris	Violin	1967	Carmarthen
Roland	Morris	Double bass	1957	Llanelli
Wynne	Morris	Violin	1985	Welshpool

Rhian	Morse	Violin	1976	Llanelli
John	Mortimer	Double bass	1967	Abergele
Iwan	Morus	Bassoon	1981	Aberystwyth
Karen	Mulcahy	Double bass	1981	Rudry
Christine	Mullins	Violin	1958	Cardiff
Linda	Mullis	Double bass	1980	Newport
Nigel	Mumford	Trombone	1953	Rhymney
Elizabeth	Murdoch	Clarinet	1973	Gowerton
Stephen	Murphy	Clarinet	1974	Barry
Cathryn	Murray	Viola	1973	Bow Street
Pat	Murray	Bassoon	1975	Rhyl
James	Mutter	Viola	1970	Cardiff
Wendy	Myhill	Viola	1973	Port Talbot
Bronwen	Naish	Cello	1956	Bodedern
Colin	Nalder	Double bass	1980	Neath
Michael	Neate	Bassoon	1978	Kenfig Hill
John	Nelson	Violin	1956	Wrexham
Scott	Newcombe	Viola	1990	Aberdare
David	Newman	Viola	1966	Bangor
Gareth	Newman	Bassoon	1966	Bangor
Elizabeth	Nicholas	Clarinet	1984	Bridgend
Lisa	Nicholas	Cello	1990	Llandysul
Elizabeth	Nicholls	Oboe	1980	Gaerwen
Max	Norman	Cello	1987	Milford Haven
Nicholas	Norman	Cello	1985	Milford Haven
Godfrey	Northam	Violin	1956	Hengoed
Matthew	Noyce	Cello	1989	Haverfordwest
Howard	Nurse	Horn	1959	Pontypridd
Jean	O'Brian	Violin	1954	Monmouth
Anthony	O'Connor	Violin	1985	Ammanford
Michael	O'Donahue	Flute	1951	Prestatyn
John	O'Hara	Percussion	1979	Llandudno
Andrew	O'Neill	Percussion	1976	Pontarddulais
Sean	O'Shea	Clarinet	1979	Porthcawl
Susanne	Oaten	Violin	1960	Cardiff
Keith	Oates	Trombone	1955	Merthyr Tydfil
Susan	Oldfield	Double bass	1982	Llanbradach
John	Oliver	Trumpet	1966	Cwmbran
Paul	Opie	Oboe	1981	Glasbury-on-Wye
Nicholas	Ormrod	Percussion	1976	Neath
Aled	Owen	Bassoon	1970	Tregarth
Catherine	Owen	Viola	1961	Bryngwran
David Gareth	Owen	Horn	1959	Brecon
Eira	Owen	Horn	1989	Montgomery
Elenid	Owen	Violin	1980	Cardiff
Eleri	Owen	Viola	1953	Llanelli
Enid	Owen	Viola	1956	Holyhead
Gwawr	Owen	Harp	1979	Llandysul
Jean	Owen	Viola	1954	Knighton
Jonathan Martin	Owen	Violin	1990	Llandegfan
Margaret Robyns	Owen	Viola	1952	Pwllheli
Martin	Owen	Violin	1988	Llandegfan
Martyn	Owen	Double bass	1976	Neath
Mary	Owen	Oboe	1953	Abertillery
Menna	Owen	Harp	1958	Glanconwy
Rachel	Owen	Percussion	1988	Caerphilly
Sharon	Owen	Trombone	1986	Cardiff
Sian	Owen	Bassoon	1977	Brynmawr
Sian	Owen	Violin	1984	Caerphilly
E. Bernard	Owens	Violin	1953	Corwen
Rachel	Owens	Percussion	1985	Caerphilly
Rhys	Owens	Trumpet	1984	Caerphilly
Sian	Owens	Violin	1979	Abertridwr
Judith	Packer	Cello	1977	Ystrad Mynach

Leila	Palmer	Violin	1951	Solva
Lucy	Paradice	Violin	1989	St Clears
Joanna	Parcell	Cello	1983	Swansea
Delyth	Pardoe	Oboe	1960	Bethesda
Korine	Parez	Violin	1990	Gowerton
Glyn	Parfitt	Viola	1951	Markham
Anne	Parker	Flute	1980	Aberystwyth
Clare	Parkholm	Cello	1987	Cardiff
David	Parr	Double bass	1966	Briton Ferry
Michael	Parrott	Cello	1960	Aberystwyth
Alison	Parry	Violin	1980	Swansea
Andrew	Parry	Violin	1969	Llandinam
Bronia	Parry	Bassoon	1975	Wrexham
Christopher	Parry	Trumpet	1981	Port Talbot
Eurof	Parry	Horn	1963	Caerau
Heledd	Parry	Violin	1985	Aberystwyth
Karen	Parry	Clarinet	1982	Colbren
Rhian Jones	Parry	Violin	1958	Wrexham
Richard	Parsons	Violin	1983	Cwmbrân
Martin	Patterson	Violin	1961	Porthcawl
Eluned	Pearce	Harp	1970	Llanddarog
Jeffrey	Pearce	Trombone	1970	Gorseinon
Andrew	Pearson	Violin	1972	Aberystwyth
Valerie	Pearson	Double bass	1960	Cwmbran
Elaine	Perrett	Violin	1974	Cardiff
Barbara	Perry	Violin	1956	Cardiff
Lesley	Perry	Violin	1956	Cardiff
Alison	Phillips	Viola	1984	Swansea
Alun	Phillips	Double bass	1958	FIshguard
Amanda Jayne	Phillips	Viola	1989	Llangyfelach
Andrew	Phillips	Violin	1978	Swansea
Ann	Phillips	Violin	1953	Dolgellau
Barbara	Phillips	Viola	1956	Haverfordwest
Catherine	Phillips	Bassoon	1982	Neath
Ceri	Phillips	Cello	1973	Aberdulais
David	Phillips	Tuba	1968	Llanelli
Denise	Phillips	Violin	1973	Sully
Dorothy	Phillips	Horn	1972	Haverfordwest
Elinor	Phillips	Double bass	1964	Ferndale
Feleiry	Phillips	Harp	1959	Aberystwyth
Gwenan	Phillips	Harp	1958	Aberystwyth
Ivor	Phillips	Clarinet	1960	Fishguard
Janet	Phillips	Violin	1952	Monmouth
Judith	Phillips	Viola	1955	Milford Haven
Justine	Phillips	Flute	1983	Cardiff
Lynne	Phillips	Violin	1976	Sully
Rachel	Phillips	Cello	1951	Milford Haven
Mona	Phipps	Viola	1957	Amlwch
Tracy	Phipps	Horn	1990	Lampeter
Joy	Pickett	Cello	1968	Goodwick
Eluned	Pierce	Horn	1971	Llanddarog
Eluned	Pierce	Harp	1974	Llanddarog
Neil	Pierce	Viola	1974	Haverfordwest
Christopher	Pigram	Trumpet	1981	Knighton
Alma	Pihlgren	Clarinet	1959	Cardiff
John	Pill	Double bass	1983	Cardiff
Sarah	Pilling	Violin	1984	Rhyl
Sian	Poncy	Double bass	1971	Neath
Christopher	Pontin	Cello	1977	Briton Ferry
Penelope	Poole	Violin	1977	Aberystwyth
Simon	Poole	Cello	1979	Aberystwyth
Christopher	Pooley	Bassoon	1952	Newport
Andrew	Popperwell	Cello	1968	Cardiff
Stephen	Popperwell	Oboe	1972	Cardiff

Reggie	Potter	Trumpet	1951	Ystalyfera
Robert	Potter	Trombone	1988	Aberystwyth
Wynneford	Potter	Viola	1980	Neath
Jill	Potts	Oboe	1978	Wrexham
John	Potts	Bassoon	1980	Wrexham
Sian	Pouncy	Double bass	1969	Neath
Anne	Powell	Violin	1954	Pontycymmer
Gwenda	Powell	Violin	1956	Wrexham
Joan	Powell	Viola	1952	Merthyr Tydfil
Julia	Powell	Viola	1983	Monmouth
Robert	Powell	Horn	1985	Aberystwyth
Janet	Prescott	Percussion	1963	Llanelli
Roger	Preston	Oboe	1966	Cardiff
Anthony	Price	Violin	1957	Cardiff
Christopher Scott	Price	Trombone	1990	Tonyrefail
Gareth	Price	Cello	1973	Comins-coch
Gareth	Price	Oboe	1982	Porthcawl
Geoffrey	Price	Violin	1960	Swansea
Helina	Price	Violin	1990	Barry
Jane	Price	Violin	1954	Ebbw Vale
Jane	Price	Violin	1974	Llandeilo
Louise	Price	Violin	1988	Port Talbot
Paul	Price	Clarinet	1986	Port Talbot
Robert	Price	Trombone	1982	Treherbert
Sian	Price	Flute	1989	Newport
Christopher	Pridd	Bassoon	1980	Newport
Anita	Priddle	Violin	1981	Cardiff
Esther	Priest	Violin	1956	Cardiff
Christopher	Prigg	Bassoon	1976	Bettws
Brian	Pritchard	Trombone	1957	Oakdale
David	Pritchard	Clarinet	1975	Pontypridd
Seona Christine	Pritchard	Viola	1987	Caergwrle
Trevor	Pritchard	Horn	1962	Holyhead
Allun	Proom	Trumpet	1977	Rogerstone
David	Prosser	Violin	1974	Merthyr Tydfil
David	Prosser	Violin	1975	Penarth
Anthony	Prothero	Violin	1979	Cardiff
Joanne	Pryce	Flute	1987	Port Talbot
John	Pryce	Cello	1964	Newtown
David	Pugh	Tuba	1959	Newtown
John	Pugh	Double bass	1966	Newtown
Nia Karen	Pugh	Violin	1989	Aberdare
Richard	Pugh	Viola	1968	Cardiff
Michael	Puttin	Horn	1951	Cardiff
Anthony	Rabbit	Violin	1975	Newport
Caroline	Rabbit	Violin	1978	Newport
Susan	Rabbit	Violin	1978	Newport
Roger	Ramsay	Cello	1977	Llanbedrog
Anthony	Randall	Horn	1953	Neath
Julia	Randall	Oboe	1972	Haverfordwest
Tony	Randall	Horn	1957	Neath
David	Rapsy	Horn	1973	Treorchy
Barbara	Rawlings	Cello	1952	Monmouth
Julia	Reardon	Violin	1979	Newport
Roy	Reece	Violin	1951	Brynaman
Adrian	Rees	Violin	1963	Port Talbot
Alan	Rees	Violin	1963	Hendy
Alun	Rees	Horn	1982	Swansea
Andrew	Rees	Violin	1977	Carmarthen
Ann Holt	Rees	Cello	1988	Carmarthen
David	Rees	Violin	1978	Carmarthen
David Hywel	Rees	Bassoon	1958	Skewen
Dulais	Rees	Viola	1970	Carmarthen
Elizabeth	Rees	Violin	1968	Gowerton

Emyr	Rees	Tuba	1982	Pont-iets
Frances	Rees	Cello	1971	Gowerton
Jane	Rees	Cello	1977	Bangor
Jeffrey	Rees	Violin	1960	Bridgend
Judith	Rees	Cello	1984	Neath
Margaret Alma	Rees	Harp	1958	Loughor
Marian	Rees	Double bass	1954	Cardiff
Nansi	Rees	Violin	1951	Wrexham
Olav	Rees	Flute	1960	Cardiff
Sharan	Rees	Violin	1970	Tenby
Stephanie	Rees	Horn	1986	Llanmorlais
Stephen	Rees	Violin	1980	Ammanford
Angus	Reid	Violin	1963	Llanelli
Frances	Rew	Violin	1979	Mathern
Mary	Reynolds	Oboe	1973	Aberdare
Neil	Reynolds	Percussion	1980	Broughton
Jonathan	Rhys	Viola	1988	Caerphilly
Leonard	Rice	Trumpet	1962	Ebbw Vale
John	Rich	Violin	1955	Risca
Ainseley	Richards	Violin	1969	Carmarthen
Bethan	Richards	Violin	1988	Aberdare
Brian	Richards	Clarinet	1968	Newtown
David	Richards	Trumpet	1953	Rhymney
David	Richards	Cello	1960	Llangefni
David	Richards	Flute	1964	Pontarddulais
David Lloyd	Richards	Cello	1961	Aberffraw
Eric	Richards	Double bass	1952	Pontarddulais
Frances	Richards	Violin	1980	Mountain Ash
Gillian	Richards	Horn	1957	Milford Haven
Huw	Richards	Harp	1985	Cowbridge
Ian	Richards	Percussion	1974	Resolfen
Janet	Richards	Cello	1955	Brecon
Louise	Richards	Violin	1983	Newport
Margaret Carys	Richards	Cello	1958	Ammanford
Robert	Richards	Trumpet	1960	Barmouth
Sarah	Richards	Oboe	1974	Swansea
Sharon	Richards	Violin	1982	Porthcawl
John	Richardson	Cello	1959	Newport
Deborah	Rickard	Violin	1978	Newport
Gillian	Ridout	Percussion	1977	Caerphilly
Kenneth	Riley	Percussion	1958	Flint
Susan	Roach	Viola	1973	Cardiff
Elen ap	Robert	Viola	1982	Cardiff
Brenda	Roberts	Percussion	1955	Caernarfon
Catherine Sian	Roberts	Violin	1989	Tonpentre
Catrin	Roberts	Flute	1977	Aberystwyth
Ceinwen	Roberts	Violin	1957	Penycae
Cynfelin	Roberts	Double bass	1951	Maesteg
Delyth	Roberts	Harp	1982	Swansea
Edward	Roberts	Violin	1963	Cardiff
Eira	Roberts	Trumpet	1985	Pontypridd
Eirion Dilwyn	Roberts	Violin	1988	Pwllheli
Eirlys	Roberts	Viola	1968	Dolgellau
Emma	Roberts	Horn	1983	Montgomery
Enid	Roberts	Clarinet	1958	Ammanford
Ffion	Roberts	Viola	1973	Llangefni
Freda	Roberts	Viola	1963	Bangor
Gareth	Roberts	Cello	1970	Welshpool
Geraint Huw	Roberts	Clarinet	1987	Rhuthun
Gerald	Roberts	Trumpet	1951	Ammanford
Graham	Roberts	Violin	1975	Newtown
Hywel Wyn	Roberts	Viola	1957	Pwllheli
Ian	Roberts	Bassoon	1963	Pontllanffraith
Iwan	Roberts	Cello	1979	Bangor

John	Roberts	Violin	1959	Beaufort
John	Roberts	Trumpet	1977	Blaenau Ffestiniog
John	Roberts	Violin	1961	Bedlinog
Katherine	Roberts	Viola	1988	Bedlinog
Keith	Roberts	Viola	1979	Cricieth
Mark	Roberts	Violin	1955	Neath
Marylyn	Roberts	Violin	1964	Penarth
Meinir	Roberts	Harp	1967	Llandysul
Michael	Roberts	Cello	1964	Newtown
Nicholas	Roberts	Double bass	1968	Colwyn Bay
Paul	Roberts	Cello	1981	Wrexham
Philip	Roberts	Violin	1959	Bedlinog
Ritchie	Roberts	Double bass	1955	Ferndale
Sarah Katherine	Roberts	Viola	1987	Treharris
Gilmour	Robinson	Bassoon	1954	Markham
Llywela	Robinson	Violin	1951	Porthmadoc
Peter	Robinson	Double bass	1978	Coychurch
Margaret Owen	Robyns	Viola	1951	Pwllheli
Julie	Roderick	Violin	1979	Gowerton
Shaun	Roderick	Bassoon	1975	Newport
John	Rodge	Cello	1970	Llwynhendy
John	Rodge	Double bass	1971	Llwynhendy
Elen Mair	Rogers	Violin	1986	Llangollen
Helen	Rogers	Viola	1990	Abergavenny
Jeanette	Rogers	Percussion	1951	Cwm
Marylyn	Rogers	Violin	1959	Sully
Philip	Rolleson	Violin	1959	Rogerstone
Tamira	Rolls	Clarinet	1989	Cardiff
David	Roose	Viola	1953	Wrexham
Andrew	Ross	Violin	1982	Newport
Jonathan	Ross	Bassoon	1977	Caerwent
Kathleen	Rouse	Violin	1957	Milford Haven
Elizabeth	Row	Clarinet	1989	Cowbridge
Enid	Rowe	Viola	1951	Cardiff
Gillian	Rowe	Double bass	1951	Abergavenny
Joy	Rowland	Double bass	1974	Port Talbot
Anne	Rowlands	Violin	1966	Llanfair Caereinion
Dyfed	Rowlands	Bassoon	1988	Aberystwyth
Gwenllian	Rowlands	Harp	1981	Ammanford
Huw Llwyd	Rowlands	Cello	1989	Aberystwyth
Jean	Rowlands	Viola	1960	Brecon
Patricia	Rowlands	Violin	1968	Llanfair Caereinon
Sioned	Rowlands	Oboe	1987	Aberystwyth
Keith	Ruddock	Violin	1956	Pontypool
Helen	Rudeforth	Horn	1980	Aberystwyth
Peter	Rudeforth	Trumpet	1982	Aberystwyth
Richard	Rugh	Viola	1967	Cardiff
David	Rule	Clarinet	1959	Pontnewydd
Ann	Rumsby	Cello	1968	Holyhead
Bernard	Russell	Flute	1963	Llanelli
Gerlad	Russell	Violin	1956	Merthyr Tydfil
Jeffrey	Ryan	Double bass	1973	Pontypridd
Philip	Ryan	Trombone	1962	Port Talbot
Jacqueline	Sadler	Percussion	1960	Cardiff
Owen	Saer	Clarinet	1987	Cardiff
Jane	Sage	Violin	1969	Cardiff
Susan	Salter	Viola	1954	Neath
John	Samuel	Violin	1956	Pontarddulais
Margaret	Samuel	Viola	1973	Merthyr Tydfil
Moroni	Samuel	Violin	1951	Llandrindod Wells
Rhian	Samuel	Oboe	1961	Aberdare
Stephen	Sanders	Percussion	1972	Newport
Alison Mary	Sangster	Double bass	1990	Ogmore-by-Sea
Brian	Sansbury	Clarinet	1967	Talybont

David	Saunders	Trombone	1972	Bridgend
Katherine	Savory	Cello	1974	Cardiff
Xiang See	Schierenberg	Violin	1985	Berriew
Deborah	Schlenther	Violin	1982	Aberystwyth
Jonathan	Schofield	Cello	1984	Newport
Karl	Scotland	Cello	1990	Cardiff
William	Scriven	Double bass	1971	Caerphilly
Nigel	Seaman	Tuba	1974	St Asaph
Janice	Seddon	Violin	1983	Broughton
John	Sephton	Cello	1957	Shotton
Brian	Sewell	Bassoon	1963	Cardiff
David	Seymour	Cello	1966	Ynysybwl
Gwyn	Seymour	Cello	1967	Ynysybwl
Patrick	Seymour	Flute	1977	Swansea
Paul	Sharrad	Horn	1986	Llangefni
David	Shaw	Violin	1955	Tonyrefail
David	Shaw	Cello	1957	Tonyrefail
Marilyn	Shearn	Violin	1967	Haverfordwest
David	Shelley	Violin	1956	Newport
Julian	Shelley	Violin	1956	Rhyl
Stuart	Shelley	Violin	1951	Rhyl
Stuart	Shelley	Violin	1953	Barry
Patricia	Sheppard	Violin	1961	Bridgend
Peter	Sheppard	Horn	1970	Bridgend
Wendy	Sheppard	Violin	1958	Bridgend
Margaret	Sherlock	Viola	1958	Barmouth
Wyndham	Sheryn	Violin	1954	Barry
Christine	Shevlan	Viola	1969	cardiff
Alan	Shimell	Double bass	1959	Barry
Doreen	Shone	Violin	1951	Hawarden
David	Short	Trombone	1984	Barry
Jennifer	Short	Viola	1966	Port Talbot
Kathryn	Short	Viola	1984	Menai Bridge
S. A.	Simon	Violin	1952	Cardiff
Christopher	Simons	Violin	1977	Penarth
Rosemary	Sims	Cello	1960	Langstone
Rosmary	Sims	Cello	1961	Ponthir
Thor	Sinclair	Violin	1982	Aberystwyth
David	Sketch	Clarinet	1962	Cardiff
Edward	Skinner	Viola	1969	Llanelli
William	Skinner	Viola	1970	Llanelli
Karen	Slade	Violin	1989	Aberystwyth
Jack M.	Slater	Violin	1951	Cardiff
Jocelyn	Slocombe	Violin	1990	Aberdare
Gareth	Small	Trumpet	1989	Swansea
Geoffrey	Smallwood	Trumpet	1954	Buckley
Melvyn	Smallwood	Trumpet	1956	Buckley
Beverley	Smith	Violin	1980	Bangor
Brian	Smith	B. Trombone	1956	Ystradgynlais
Christopher	Smith	Cello	1985	Bangor
Ian	Smith	Horn	1975	Bow Street
Joanne	Smith	Violin	1985	Llandybïe
Justin	Smith	Clarinet	1959	Cardiff
Katie	Smith	Violin	1982	Bangor
Ralph	Smith	Cello	1982	Swansea
Rosemary	Smith	Violin	1974	Cardiff
Wendy	Smith	Viola	1961	Newport
Catherine	Spalding	Violin	1958	Wrexham
Jane	Spalding	Violin	1959	Wrexham
Nyree	Spark	Viola	1986	Pontardawe
Tim	Spear	Trombone	1987	Cardiff
Martin	Spencer	Viola	1985	Caerphilly
John	Spicer	Double bass	1964	Kenfig Hill
Patricia	Spillane	Viola	1971	Milford Haven

Hilary	Squire	Violin	1951	Neath
J. Mansel	Squire	Oboe	1953	Skewen
Sharon	Stace	Violin	1985	Manorbier
Sharon	Stace	Flute	1988	Monorbier
Edward	Staneham	Bassoon	1955	Newport
Philip	Stead	Tuba	1985	Cardiff
Hugo	Steiner	Violin	1982	Gelligaer
Garth	Stephens	Flute	1959	Bargoed
Keith	Stephens	Violin	1964	Risca
Judith	Stiles	Violin	1964	Cardiff
Bernard	Stirrup	Violin	1951	Pontarddulais
Philip	Stokes	Violin	1963	Blaenavon
Terence	Strachan	Viola	1951	Merthyr Tydfil
John	Stradling	Trombone	1963	Usk
Naomi	Stray	Bassoon	1953	Rossett
Alison	Street	Flute	1981	Ponthir
Elizabeth	Street	Cello	1966	Neath
Roger	Strong	Violin	1956	Cardiff
Kate	Studman	Flute	1989	Llandridnod Wells
Sian	Stumbles	Violin	1972	Llandrindod Wells
Robert	Suff	Oboe	1982	Swansea
Wendy	Sullivan	Cello	1980	Neath
Carys	Swain	Harp	1988	Llantrisant
Robert	Swain	Violin	1964	Pontypridd
Patricia	Swales	Clarinet	1963	Haverfordwest
David	Swanson	Trombone	1976	Guilsfield
Desmond	Sweeney	Violin	1951	Swansea
Michael	Syrett	Bassoon	1960	Whitchurch
Pippa	Syrett	Viola	1984	Reynoldston
Edwina	Talbot	Viola	1969	Milford Haven
Penelope	Talbot	Viola	1971	Penarth
Hilary	Tann	Cello	1963	Ferndale
Ruth	Tatevossian	Violin	1989	Cardiff
Barry	Taylor	Cello	1973	Newtown
Caroline	Taylor	Violin	1979	Swansea
Edgar	Taylor	Horn	1954	Cardiff
Michael	Taylor	Trombone	1958	Pontardawe
Pauline	Taylor	Viola	1964	Merthyr Tydfil
Sonia	Taylor	Violin	1970	Llangefni
Myfanwy	Tayson	Violin	1961	Llanelli
Geraint	Tellen	Violin	1983	Bridgend
Stuart	Telling	Viola	1964	Nelson
Mark	Terry	Double bass	1982	Cwmbrân
Alan	Thomas	Double bass	1954	Neath
Alan	Thomas	Cello	1961	Bridgend
Alan	Thomas	Violin	1983	Merthyr Tydfil
Alun	Thomas	Violin	1958	Ammanford
Alun	Thomas	Trombone	1959	Merthyr Tydfil
Alun	Thomas	Violin	1978	Merthyr Tydfil
Alun	Thomas	Oboe	1984	Swansea
Ann	Thomas	Double bass	1961	Horton
Anne Veronica	Thomas	Flute	1960	Porthcawl
Arthur Robert	Thomas	Cello	1960	Loughor
Avril	Thomas	Violin	1966	Bridgend
Bryan	Thomas	Violin	1958	Clydach
Bryn	Thomas	Trumpet	1961	Llandeilo
Carol	Thomas	Violin	1975	Llandeilo
Caryl	Thomas	Harp	1975	Carmarthen
Catrin	Thomas	Oboe	1971	Cardigan
Catrin	Thomas	Clarinet	1972	Cardigan
Catrin	Thomas	Cello	1980	Borth
Christine	Thomas	Cello	1961	Haverfordwest
Christopher	Thomas	Percussion	1982	Penarth
Clive	Thomas	Violin	1951	Gowerton

D. Michael	Thomas	Viola	1953	Whitland
David	Thomas	Violin	1957	Rhosllannerchrugog
David	Thomas	Violin	1964	Aberystwyth
David	Thomas	Violin	1967	Pontarddulais
David	Thomas	Bassoon	1975	Newtown
David O.	Thomas	Viola	1958	Fishguard
David W.	Thomas	Violin	1959	Rhos
Dewi	Thomas	Viola	1966	Tregaron
Edward J.	Thomas	Trumpet	1951	Haverfordwest
Edwina	Thomas	Viola	1973	Gowerton
Einion	Thomas	Trombone	1970	Harlech
Elaine	Thomas	Clarinet	1983	Briton Ferry
Elen	Thomas	Viola	1963	Bangor
Elin	Thomas	Viola	1964	Llanelen
Elizabeth	Thomas	Violin	1952	Dolgellau
Emlyn	Thomas	Trombone	1951	Pontarddulais
Frances	Thomas	Cello	1959	Dolgellau
Gareth	Thomas	Viola	1970	Colwyn Bay
Garth ap	Thomas	Flute	1958	Gaerwen
Geoffrey	Thomas	Viola	1966	Gorseinon
George L.	Thomas	Violin	1957	Aberdare
Glenda R.	Thomas	Violin	1957	Swansea
Grace Mansel	Thomas	Cello	1959	Llandough
Guto	Thomas	Violin	1989	Cardiff
Gwenfair	Thomas	Viola	1966	Bangor
Gwynallt	Thomas	Cello	1953	Pontarddulais
Haward	Thomas	Cello	1956	Pontarddulais
Heather	Thomas	Clarinet	1978	Wrexham
Heulwen	Thomas	Violin	1977	Llanarth
Howard	Thomas	Cello	1957	Pontarddulais
Hugh	Thomas	Violin	1953	Llanelli
Hugh	Thomas	Percussion	1977	Llanelli
Hugh	Thomas	Violin	1981	Swansea
Hugh	Thomas	Violin	1952	Borth
Huw	Thomas	Percussion	1975	Aberystwyth
Huw	Thomas	Trombone	1980	Cardiff
Hywel	Thomas	Clarinet	1958	Merthyr Tydfil
Ioan	Thomas	Viola	1957	Penclawdd
J. Edward	Thomas	Trumpet	1952	Haverfordwest
J. Emlyn M.	Thomas	Trombone	1952	Pontarddulais
Janette ap	Thomas	Viola	1957	Llanddaniel
Jean	Thomas	Harp	1953	Llandeilo
Jennifer	Thomas	Flute	1964	Wrexham
Jennifer	Thomas	Flute	1968	Swansea
John Roger	Thomas	Viola	1958	Loughor
Jonathan	Thomas	Viola	1986	Caerphilly
Joseph	Thomas	Clarinet	1962	Swansea
Julia	Thomas	Bassoon	1985	Penarth
Kathryn	Thomas	Cello	1975	Cardigan
Lyn	Thomas	Percussion	1962	Felinfoel
Lyn	Thomas	Percussion	1963	Llanelli
Lynne	Thomas	Violin	1987	Porthcawl
Madlen	Thomas	Viola	1968	Llanelli
Maelgwyn	Thomas	Flute	1967	Bangor
Margaret Lyn	Thomas	Percussion	1961	Felinfoel
Mark	Thomas	Violin	1972	Penclawdd
Megan	Thomas	Violin	1952	Skewen
Megan	Thomas	Violin	1973	Abercrave
Meirion	Thomas	Clarinet	1963	Swansea
Meurig	Thomas	Viola	1979	Llangefni
Michael	Thomas	Viola	1963	Carmarthen
Myra	Thomas	Viola	1955	Milford Haven
Pat	Thomas	Cello	1951	Hakin
Peter	Thomas	Percussion	1981	Swansea

Phillip	Thomas	Percussion	1972	Neath
Rebecca	Thomas	Violin	1988	Neath
Rhian	Thomas	Oboe	1963	Cardiff
Rhian	Thomas	Violin	1980	Borth
Richard	Thomas	Horn	1966	Gaerwen
Rona	Thomas	Flute	1954	Wrexham
Ruth	Thomas	Percussion	1959	Port Talbot
Sara	Thomas	Cello	1977	Glyncoch
Sheanna	Thomas	Flute	1984	Caerleon
Siân Mansel	Thomas	Viola	1959	Llandough
Simon	Thomas	Violin	1976	Llanelli
Susan	Thomas	Flute	1986	Merthyr Tydfil
Sylvia	Thomas	Viola	1959	Barry
W. Hugh	Thomas	Violin	1955	Llanelli
Walter	Thomas	Oboe	1959	Neath
William Clive	Thomas	Violin	1952	Gowerton
Wyndham	Thomas	Violin	1955	Bridgend
Justin	Thorogood	Trombone	1985	Cardiff
James	Timothy	Violin	1974	Newport
Robert	Timothy	Viola	1976	Newport
Robert	Tonkin	Violin	1972	Gowerton
Anne-Marie	Treharne	Violin	1978	Llanelli
Christopher	Treharne	Violin	1975	Llanelli
Cynthia	Tse	Oboe	1986	Abergavenny
Julia	Tuckett	Cello	1979	Treorchy
Yvonne	Tuckett	Double bass	1976	Treorchy
Gavin	Tudball	Cello	1985	Penygraig
Gareth	Tudor	Viola	1980	Abertridwr
Jane	Tunley	Violin	1975	Ebbw Vale
Susan	Tunley	Violin	1976	Ebbw Vale
Lorna	Turk	Violin	1983	Cwmbran
Simone Claire	Turner	Cello	1987	Saltney
Susan	Turner	Viola	1971	Cardiff
David	Tyler	Trombone	1982	Cwmbran
Vivien	Tyler	Violin	1975	Llantarnam
David	Valentine	Cello	1987	St David's
Pauline	Vaughan	Horn	1984	Newtown
Alan	Verheyden	Violin	1966	Swansea
Jill	Veyzey	Violin	1958	Abercarn
Tim	Vinall	Trumpet	1985	Cardiff
David	Walker	Violin	1972	Merthyr Tydfil
Geoffrey	Walker	Bassoon	1956	Monmouth
Catherine	Wallace	Flute	1978	Newport
Richard	Wallace	Viola	1974	Newport
Susan	Walrond-Skinner	Violin	1959	Langstone
Ann	Walter	Cello	1954	Monmouth
Aled	Walters	Trumpet	1990	Cardiff
Arwyn	Walters	Violin	1954	Pontlliw
Elizabeth	Walters	Cello	1959	Caerphilly
Emyr	Walters	Violin	1960	Neath
Jacqueline	Walters	Violin	1971	Pontarddulais
Julian	Walters	Double bass	1989	Neath
Lee	Walters	Violin	1969	Hendy
Ruth	Walters	Violin	1973	Aberystwyth
T. Arwyn	Walters	Violin	1955	Pontlliw
Joan	Ward	Violin	1961	Merthyr Tydfil
John	Ward	Bassoon	1961	Briton Ferry
Myra	Ward	Double bass	1952	Newport
Wayne	Warlow	Cello	1957	Pontypridd
Kathleen Ann	Washington	Cello	1987	Newtown
Robert	Waters	Clarinet	1957	Cardiff
Roderick	Waters	Oboe	1964	Newport
Christopher	Watkins	Double bass	1966	Newtown
Delyth	Watkins	Double bass	1952	Ammanford

Dewi	Watkins	Cello	1967	Caerphilly
Jeffery	Watkins	Double bass	1964	Newtown
John	Watkins	Viola	1959	Newbridge
Julia	Watkins	Violin	1975	Brynmawr
Kenneth	Watkins	Violin	1960	Llandeilo
Nigel	Watkins	Double bass	1980	Penclawdd
Paul	Watkins	Cello	1982	Blackwood
Jane	Watts	Violin	1976	St Dogmaels
David	Wayne	Oboe	1975	Cefn Cribwr
David	Weakley	Trombone	1967	Cardiff
Alasdair	Weaks	Tuba	1980	Pontyberem
Elizabeth	Weale	Violin	1967	Llandrindod Wells
Hywel Francis	Webley	Violin	1989	Merthyr Tydfil
Joan	Webster	Violin	1966	Wrexham
Christopher	Weeks	Clarinet	1964	Penlle'r-gaer
John	Weeks	Flute	1960	Penllergaer
Richard	Weiser	Violin	1957	Swansea
Michael	Welsby	Double bass	1974	Caerphilly
William	Weston	Double bass	1986	Hawarden
Keith	Westwood	Clarinet	1954	Neath
John	Wetherall	Horn	1972	Cardiff
Graham	White	Double bass	1968	Caerleon
Graham	White	Cello	1970	Cwmbran
Haydn	White	Trombone	1957	Ystradgynlais
Walter J.	White	Trumpet	1953	Ystradgymais
Andrew Thomas	Whitehead	Violin	1987	Aberdare
Hannah	Whitehouse	Violin	1959	Porthcawl
Sarah	Whitehouse	Cello	1960	Porthcawl
Tom	Whitehouse	Flute	1961	Porthcawl
Paul	Whittaker	Percussion	1973	Wrexham
Christopher	Whitten	Percussion	1975	Abergavenny
Richard	Wiegold	Cello	1983	Caerphilly
Richard	Wieser	Violin	1956	Swansea
Dorothy	Wilbraham	Horn	1956	Beddgelert
Stephen	Wild	Horn	1981	Porthcawl
Richard	Wilde	Violin	1976	Bridgend
Mary	Wilkie	Violin	1955	Denbigh
Kate	Wilkinson	Clarinet	1976	Swansea
Adrian	Williams	Violin	1969	Croesyceiliog
Alun	Williams	Trumpet	1975	Ebbw Vale
Alun	Williams	Horn	1981	Ystrad Mynach
Andrea	Williams	Violin	1987	Newport
Andrew	Williams	Flute	1956	Cardiff
Andrew	Williams	Trombone	1990	Penarth
Annwyl	Williams	Oboe	1961	Llanelli
Barbara	Williams	Violin	1969	Llanelli
Beryl	Williams	Violin	1963	Llangefni
Bethan	Williams	Harp	1963	Rhuthun
Catrin	Williams	Harp	1984	St Asaph
Christine	Williams	Viola	1959	Cardiff
Claire	Williams	Violin	1990	Pontarddulais
D. Michael	Williams	Violin	1964	Aberystwyth
Daryl	Williams	Trumpet	1968	Cwmbrân
David	Williams	Trombone	1954	Ynyshir
David	Williams	Violin	1961	Swansea
David	Williams	Cello	1964	Tylorstown
David	Williams	Horn	1977	Pontypridd
David C.	Williams	Violin	1963	Port Talbot
David Geraint	Williams	Trombone	1988	Aberdare
David H.	Williams	Violin	1963	Swansea
David I.	Williams	Trombone	1953	Ynyshir
David John	Williams	Cello	1952	Caerphilly
David Lloyd	Williams	Harp	1986	Carmel
David M.	Williams	Violin	1961	Llanrwst

David M. L.	Williams	Double bass	1952	Grovesend
Elen Sian	Williams	Violin	1989	Bala
Elenid	Williams	Violin	1956	Llanelli
Elizabeth	Williams	Violin	1951	Camrose
Enid	Williams	Viola	1957	Merthyr Tydfil
Enid	Williams	Violin	1960	Llangefni
Gareth	Williams	Violin	1966	Llangefni
Gareth	Williams	Viola	1969	Colwyn Bay
Gareth	Williams	Horn	1984	Aberdare
Gareth Wyn	Williams	Double bass	1987	Clydach
Geraint	Williams	Double bass	1985	Taff's Well
Geraint R.	Williams	Double bass	1986	Taff's Well
Gethin H.	Williams	Viola	1952	Llanelli
Glenys	Williams	Cello	1956	Beaumaris
Glyn	Williams	Violin	1951	Buckley
Glyn	Williams	Bassoon	1973	Abergele
Gregory	Williams	Viola	1967	Gresford
Gwennan	Williams	Viola	1979	Mold
Gwyn	Williams	Trumpet	1966	Llangefni
Hugh	Williams	Horn	1975	Llanfairfechan
Huw	Williams	Cello	1974	Lampeter
Huw	Williams	Horn	1976	Llanfairfechan
Ian	Williams	Horn	1976	Pontypridd
Ian	Williams	Double bass	1979	Coedpoeth
J. Eifion	Williams	Clarinet	1951	Morriston
Jane	Williams	Cello	1974	Cardiff
Janet	Williams	Violin	1975	Llanelli
Janet	Williams	Clarinet	1984	Boughton
Janet Norma	Williams	Clarinet	1986	Bickley
Janet Sheila	Williams	Viola	1959	Cwmbran
Jayne	Williams	Violin	1984	Cardiff
Joan	Williams	Violin	1968	Llangefni
John	Williams	Trumpet	1959	Godre'r-graig
John	Williams	Viola	1960	Cemais
John	Williams	Cello	1970	Seven Sisters
John F.	Williams	Horn	1951	Cardiff
John Frederick	Williams	Horn	1952	Cardiff
Jonathan	Williams	Clarinet	1961	Neath
Jonathan	Williams	Horn	1986	Cardiff
Julian	Williams	Percussion	1984	Llanelli
Keith	Williams	Clarinet	1952	Buckley
Keith	Williams	Clarinet	1955	Rhyl
Keith	Williams	Violin	1956	Merthyr Tydfil
Mair	Williams	Violin	1967	Llangefni
Malcolm	Williams	Double bass	1951	Grovesend
Margaret	Williams	Viola	1952	Merthyr Tydfil
Margaret	Williams	Harp	1960	Llandudno
Mark	Williams	Trumpet	1979	Llandudno
Martyn Graeme	Williams	Trombone	1988	Denbigh
Mary	Williams	Violin	1964	Llanelli
Mary	Williams	Violin	1967	Llangefni
Mary-Claire	Williams	Violin	1990	Bridgend
Meirion	Williams	Cello	1968	Seven Sisters
Menna	Williams	Violin	1959	Pontarddulais
Michael	Williams	Violin	1960	Ammanford
Michael	Williams	Violin	1963	Aberystwyth
Nigel	Williams	Viola	1964	Newtown
Patricia	Williams	Viola	1961	Haverfordwest
Paul	Williams	Cello	1979	Bridgend
Penelope	Williams	Violin	1967	Cardiff
Quentin	Williams	Cello	1957	Llangennech
Quentin	Williams	Double bass	1961	Llangennech
Rebecca	Williams	Violin	1984	Saundersfoot
Rhian	Williams	Harp	1980	Aberystwyth

Rhodri	Williams	Clarinet	1972	Lampeter
Richard Ll.	Williams	Violin	1959	Llanfyllin
Robin	Williams	Violin	1961	Llangennech
Roger	Williams	Viola	1958	Llanelli
Sharon	Williams	Violin	1986	Neath
Sian Ellis	Williams	Clarinet	1966	Holyhead
Sioned	Williams	Harp	1970	Mold
Stephanie	Williams	Viola	1981	Rhyl
Stephen	Williams	Double bass	1976	Brynmenyn
Steven	Williams	Tuba	1975	Aberdare
Susan	Williams	Viola	1973	Michaelston-super-Ely
Susannah	Williams	Viola	1977	Brecon
Valerie	Williams	Horn	1952	Cardiff
Wynford	Williams	Violin	1963	Ammanford
Catherine	Wilshaw	Viola	1984	Haverfordwest
Corolyn	Wilson	Oboe	1954	Swansea
Madeline	Wilson	Trumpet	1968	Newbridge
Andrienna	Windmill	Horn	1990	Pontypridd
Katherine	Wishaw	Viola	1983	Haverfordwest
Mary	Wojsik	Violin	1956	Llangefni
Gareth	Wood	Double bass	1968	Pontypridd
Vernon	Wood	Violin	1951	Porth
Brian	Woodgate	Violin	1958	Cardiff
Jennifer	Woodman	Double bass	1959	Newport
Colin	Woolmer	Viola	1985	Milford Haven
Sarah	Worsley	Violin	1980	Denbigh
Graham	Worth	Trumpet	1983	Cardiff
Alison Joanne	Wright	Flute	1990	Mold
Gemma	Wright	Violin	1985	Llangoed
Ian	Wright	Violin	1981	Narberth
Liza	Wright	Cello	1989	Hengoed
Rosemary	Wright	Violin	1972	Cardiff
Wendy	Wright	Percussion	1986	Llandudno
Helen	Wvans	Viola	1976	Cardiff
Rhodri	Wyn	Oboe	1985	Aberystwyth
Manon	Wyn Parry	Harp	1985	Y Groeslon
Helen	Wynn Jones	Violin	1982	Llandeilo
Sian	Wynne	Violin	1985	Swansea
Brian	Yates	Violin	1960	Cardiff
Robert	Yates	Double bass	1973	Carmarthen
Gary	Young	Trombone	1983	Swansea
Margaret	Young	Oboe	1986	Swansea

Appendix III: Landmarks in the Orchestra's Development

1946 First concert at the Rolls Hall, Monmouth.

1948 First appearance at the National Eisteddfod of Wales where the first recordings were made for future broadcasting.

1953 First broadcast to the Commonwealth to mark the Coronation of Queen Elizabeth II.

First television appearance – from Rhyl National Eisteddfod.

1955 The National Youth Orchestra of Wales appeared at the Edinburgh Festival.

1956 First record launched by Qualiton Records.

1957 The Orchestra undertook its first concert tour abroad.

Appendix IV: National Youth Orchestra of Wales Recordings

1951   Conducted by Clarence Raybould. *Ruy Blas* Overture (Mendelssohn); *Water Music* (Handel); 'From Bohemia's Woods and Fields' (Smetana); *Sospiri* (Elgar); Symphony No. 4: finale (Brahms). Mecoligo Records CNBL/1/11, FNBL/2/10, CNBL/3/9, CNBL/1/8, CNBL/2/6, CNBL/3/7 (all 78s).

1956   Conducted by Clarence Raybould. *New World Symphony* (Dvořák). Qualiton Records, QLP 1000.

1969   Conducted by Arthur Davison. Fanfare (Walton, arr. Sargent); 'Hen Wlad Fy Nhadau' (arr. David Wynne); Welsh Dances, Suite No. 2 Op. 64 (Alun Hoddinott); *Finlandia* (Sibelius); Fantasia on Welsh Nursery Tunes (Grace Williams); Trumpet Voluntary (J. Clarke, arr. Henry Wood; soloist Gwyn Williams); *Le Carnaval Romain* Overture (Berlioz). MFP Stereo 2129.

1973   Conducted by Arthur Davison. *Pictures at an Exhibition* (Mussorgsky); *Festival Overture* (1954) (Shostakovitch). MFP 57009.

1975   Conducted by Arthur Davison. Welsh Dances Suite No. 2 Op. 64 (Alun Hoddinott); Sinfonietta Op. 34 (William Mathias); Investiture Dances Op. 66 (Hoddinott); Concerto Grosso No. 2 Op. 46 (Hoddinott); Celtic Dances Op. 60 (Mathias). BBC Records and Tapes (Welsh Arts Council), REC 222 Stereo.

Select Bibliography

David Allsobrook, *Music for Wales*, Cardiff, 1992.

A. Camden, *Blow by Blow*, London, 1982.

H. C. Colles, *Walford Davies*, London, 1942.

P. Crossley-Holland (ed.), *Music in Wales*, London, 1948.

E. L. Ellis, *TJ, A Life of Dr Thomas Jones, CH*, Cardiff, 1992.

J. G. Evans and Alun John, 'Rae Jenkins, 1903–1985 – two tributes', *Welsh Music*, 8, 3, 1986.

Daniel Jones, *Music in Wales*, Cardiff, 1961.

Kenneth Loveland, 'The Welsh Musical Awakening', *Welsh Music*, II, 8, 1965.

Ian Parrott, *Walford Davies*, London, 1942.

Ian Parrott, *The Spiritual Pilgrims*, Narberth and Tenby, 1964.

R. Railton, *Daring to Excel: The Story of the National Youth Orchestra of Great Britain*, London, 1992.

Alec Strahan, 'Les Jeunesses Musicales de France', *Musical Times*, February 1950.

D. Taylor, *Music Now*, Milton Keynes, 1979.

Gareth Williams, 'How's the tenors in Dowlais?: hegemony, harmony and popular culture in England and Wales, 1600–1900', *Llafur*, 5, 1, 1988.

Grace Williams, 'Gareth Walters', *Welsh Music*, I, 8, 1961.

Index